# Irish Theatre International

EDITORIAL GROUP

EDITOR
Paul Murphy
Queen's University Belfast
p.murphy@qub.ac.uk

EDITORIAL ASSISTANTS
Trish McTighe, Queen's University Belfast
Emma O'Kane, Queen's University Belfast
Conor Plunkett, Queen's University Belfast

DESIGN CONSULTANT
Kurt Taroff, Queen's University Belfast

IRISH LANGUAGE CONSULTANT
Charles Dillon, Queen's University Belfast

EDITORIAL ADVISORY BOARD

Nicholas Grene, Trinity College Dublin, Republic of Ireland
Cheryl Herr, University of Iowa, USA
Joan Fitzpatrick Dean, University of Missouri-Kansas City, USA
Janelle Reinelt, University of Warwick, UK
Marilynn Richtarik, Georgia State University, USA
Anthony Roche, University College Dublin, Republic of Ireland
Shaun Richards, Staffordshire University, UK
Neil Sammells, Bath Spa University College, UK
Brian Singleton, Trinity College Dublin, Republic of Ireland

*Irish Theatre International* is published by Carysfort Press for the Irish Society for Theatre Research

HOW TO ORDER

TRADE ORDERS DIRECTLY TO:
Columba Mercier Distribution,
55A Spruce Avenue,
Stillorgan Industrial Park,
Blackrock,
Co.Dublin
T: (353 1) 294 2560
F: (353 1) 294 2564
E: cmd@columba.ie

FOR SALES IN NORTH AMERICA AND CANADA:
Dufour Editions Inc.,
124 Byers Road,
PO Box 7,
Chester Springs, PA 19425,
USA
T:1-610-458-5005
F:1-610-458-7103
E: info@dufoureditions.com

Published by Carysfort Press Ltd, 58 Woodfield, Scholarstown Road, Dublin 16, Ireland

ISBN  978-1-78874-891-9
ISSN  2009-0870

Printed and bound by eprint limited Unit 35, Coolmine Industrial Estate, Dublin 15, Ireland

## Instructions for Contributors

### Editorial Policy
Irish Theatre International, the peer-reviewed journal of ISTR, publishes research on Irish theatre in its national and international contexts in terms of an engagement with the full spectrum of Irish theatre from page to stage; and research on interdisciplinary research between theatre studies in Ireland and the wider community of theatre and performance studies in its international contexts.

### Submissions
Articles in English submitted for publication should be sent to Dr Paul Murphy, Editor, Irish Theatre International, Drama Department, School of Languages, Literatures & Performing Arts, Queen's University, Belfast, BT7 1NN, Northern Ireland. The Editor should preferably be contacted at p.murphy@qub.ac.uk. Submission of a paper will be taken to imply that it is unpublished and is not being considered for publication elsewhere. Contributors are responsible for obtaining permission to reproduce any materials, including photographs and illustrations for which they do not hold copyright.

### Manuscript preparation
The recommended length for articles is 4000-6000 words. An electronic copy of the manuscript in WORD should be submitted to the above email address. The author's name, address, email address, and title of manuscript should appear on a separate cover sheet. An abstract of no more than 150 words should also be included as well as a brief biography. Please note that articles which do not conform to the Text Conventions detailed below will NOT be published.

### Text Conventions
1. Articles must be typed and double-spaced throughout. Quotations and Notes are also double-spaced. Do not exceed 35 lines per page nor 70 characters per line.
2. Leave margins of 1" (25mm) at right, top and bottom, and a larger margin of 1. 112" (40mm) on left.
3. Italicize titles of books, newspapers, journals.
4. Titles of articles are given in single quotation marks.
5. Notes are indicated by raised Arabic numerals (without any other sign) at the end of the sentence, following any punctuation.1 Notes are numbered in sequence throughout the article.2
6. Use English (Oxford) spelling for your own text, but give the original spelling in quotations (archaic, American...).
7. Write ... ize and ... ization. Not ... ise, ...isation.
8. No full stop after Dr, Mr, Mrs, and similar abbreviations ending with the same letter as the full form. Other abbreviations take the full stop (Esq., p.m.,...), except capitals used in abbreviations of journals (PMLA, TLS) or of organizations (UNESCO).
9. For dates, use only the form 15 May 1985.
10. Write out in full 'do not', 'will not', etc. ...
11. Use minimal numerals: 1985-6, 1888-92, 141-2, but 13-15, 111-19.
12. Write: 'ninety nine spectators', but '101 fans'.
13. 'Act III, sc. v, lines 35-51' becomes after a quotation: (III,v: 35-51). For volume, or part, use roman numerals: I, II...
14. Write centuries in full. Hyphenate the adjectival use: 'seventeenth-century drama', but 'the theatre in the seventeenth century...'
15. Seventies or 1970s (no apostrophe).
16. Possessive case: as a rule, write 's.
17. Do not forget to number your pages.
18. Illustrations are indicated in the text thus: (Fig. 1). When submitting illustrations, please include comprehensive captions, drawing the reader's attention to the important features of each picture. It is your responsibility to obtain permission for the reproduction in Irish Theatre International of photographic or other illustrative materials. List the captions at the end of your document, prefaced by 'Fig. 1', etc. The captions should refer to the text and NOT list simply character names, etc. Photographers must be credited.
19. If in doubt, please refer to the MHRA (Modern Humanities Research Association) Style Guide: www.mhra.org.uk/Publications/Books/StyleGuide/index.html.
20. NOTES/REFERENCES: Make all references in endnotes according to the following conventions:
**Book**: Christopher Murray, *Sean O'Casey: Writer at Work: A Biography* (Dublin: Gill and Macmillan, 2004), p. 261.
**Chapter in book**: Mary C. King, 'J.M. Synge, "national" drama and the post-Protestant imagination' in Shaun Richards, ed., *The Cambridge Companion to Twentieth Century Irish Drama* (Cambridge: Cambridge University Press, 2004), pp. 79-92.
**Journal article**: Anna McMullan, 'Masculinity and Masquerade in Tom Kilroy's Double Cross and The Secret Fall of Constance Wilde,' *Irish University Review*, 32: 1 (2002), pp. 126-136.
**Newspaper article**: Fintan O'Toole, 'Murderous Laughter', *Irish Times*, 24 June 1997.
Repeat references with author's name and page number, and if there are several references to the same author include short reference to title as well.

# Contents

2    Editorial
     **PAUL MURPHY**


**ARTICLES**

4    'More real for Northern Irish Catholics than anybody else':
     Brian Friel's Earliest Plays
     **SCOTT BOLTWOOD**

16   Brian Friel, Tyrone Guthrie and Thornton Wilder
     **CHRISTOPHER MURRAY**

28   Changing the Direction of Theatre:
     Brian Friel's *Crystal and Fox* and John Osborne's *The Entertainer*
     **ANTHONY ROCHE**

38   Brian Friel and the Sovereignty of Language
     **NICHOLAS GRENE**

48   Space in *Wonderful Tennessee*
     **HELEN LOJEK**

62   *The Home Place*: Unhomely Inheritances
     **ANNA MCMULLAN**

Irish Theatre International, Vol. 2, No. 1, pp. 2-3

# Editorial

PAUL MURPHY

In terms of Irish theatre, Brian Friel is perhaps the most internationally acclaimed playwright of his generation. It is appropriate then that in his 80th year this issue of *Irish Theatre International* focuses specifically on Friel's dramatic canon. The articles in this issue reflect the range and calibre of Friel's work, covering his earliest plays from *The Blind Mice* (1963), through to his magnum opus *Translations* (1980) and up to his most recent work to date *The Home Place* (2005).

Scott Boltwood engages with Friel's earlier work, charting his development as a playwright in terms of his radio plays and his first plays for the stage. Boltwood considers Friel's earliest plays within the context of the Ulster theatre tradition and specifically argues for the importance of *The Blind Mice* for a new understanding of Friel's early career. Christopher Murray suggests that in the congruence of like minds Friel educated himself in the best modern theatrical production values by looking for models to Tyrone Guthrie and Thornton Wilder at the same time. Murray defines a triangular relationship between the dramaturgy of Friel, Guthrie and Wilder within which Friel's stagecraft might be looked at anew.

Anthony Roche contends that although the connection between Friel and that of Russian playwrights Chekhov and Turgenev has been well flagged, not least by the playwright himself, what has rarely been noted is his creative engagement with British theatre of the mid-twentieth century. Roche delineates a context in the wake of the Belfast agreement, in which critics are beginning to speak more openly of Friel's dialogue with contemporaneous British playwrights. In terms of this critical context Roche offers an intertextual comparison of Friel's *Crystal and Fox* (1968), and John Osborne's *The Entertainer* (1957). Nicholas Grene suggests that in spite of Friel's reverence for the superior expressiveness of music, and in spite of his awareness of the deficiencies of the word, Friel creates a theatre dependent on the persuasive powers of language. Grene argues that if they are to be held in Friel's theatre an audience must, at key moments, trust in language and go with its flow. Grene contends that it is language at such points, not music, not dance, that is sovereign in Friel's plays.

Helen Lojek notes that Friel's most familiar plays are generally set in indoor space; often the indoor space is juxtaposed to contiguous exterior space or to fluid, shifting space, but Friel's stages typically present us with enclosed space that suggests norms about who may occupy that space and how they should behave. Lojek argues that in *Wonderful Tennessee* (1993) Friel uses an exterior setting to situate characters in space less familiar to them and unlikely to play a regular role in their lives. Lojek suggests that Friel's use of space highlights the vulnerability and freedom of the characters, but also the extent to which actions that occur there constitute an interlude in their lives rather than a quotidian reality. Anna McMullan engages with Friel's latest play *The Home Place*, specifically in terms of its 2009 production by the Lyric Theatre at the Grand Opera House in Belfast. McMullan engages with such dramaturgical issues as to what extent Friel uses theatrical conventions, particularly on and off stage, appearances and disappearances, to raise questions about inheritances imposed or lost, and related questions of possession and dispossession, home and displacement.

I must express my thanks to all those scholars who were kind enough to read submissions and provide peer-review reports in good time, and to all the members of the Editorial Advisory Board for their support. I am very grateful to Eamonn Jordan and Carysfort Press for their support in producing the journal, and also to the Arts Council Ireland/An Chomhairle Ealaíon. My thanks as always to my colleague Kurt Taroff for his technical expertise. I am also grateful to Trish McTighe, Emma O'Kane and Conor Plunkett for their assistance in editing this special issue of *Irish Theatre International*.

It is with sadness that I must note the passing of Desmond Ernest Stewart Maxwell who died earlier this year. Desmond was a distinguished scholar who made an enormous contribution to the study of Irish theatre in such books as *A Critical History of Irish Drama: 1891-1980* (1984), and notably *Brian Friel* (1973), the first major study of Friel's plays. It is only fitting that this issue of *Irish Theatre International* is dedicated to the memory of DES Maxwell.

Irish Theatre International, Vol. 2, No. 1, pp. 4-15
©Irish Society for Theatre Research, 2009. Printed in the Republic of Ireland.

'More real for Northern Irish Catholics than anybody else':
Brian Friel's Earliest Plays

Scott Boltwood

*A full survey of Brian Friel's eight withdrawn plays of the 1960s for television, radio, and the stage has not been attempted since Ulf Dantanus's comprehensive treatment of 1989, and future scholars would find the task especially daunting because of the general unavailability of these works. While the National Library of Ireland houses Friel's collected papers — containing one-hundred-thirty boxes of manuscripts, correspondence, contracts, and diverse production ephemera — the Friel Papers focus overwhelmingly on the stage plays. In other words, the documents that would allow scholars to reconstruct a comprehensive assessment of his early career are absent: his* Irish Press *articles, screen plays, essays, and much of the ancillary material for his minor works. Such a survey is beyond the scope of this essay as well; however, the intention is to consider Friel's earliest plays within the context of the Ulster theatre tradition and, specifically, to argue for the importance of* The Blind Mice *for a new understanding of Friel's early career.*

On 20th February 2009, Queen's University, Belfast, announced the inauguration of the Brian Friel Theatre and Centre for Theatre Research. For a man who stated in 1963 that Northern Ireland was ruled by 'that rotten mob [...] those sadistic thugs' and moved to the Republic in 1967, Friel's endorsement of such a Northern Ireland institution publicly signaled his reconciliation with his former homeland.[1] In his earliest interviews, he famously stated that he was a nationalist and aspired to write the 'great Irish play,' and despite his tenure with the Field Day Theatre Company during the 1980s, he has been associated with the Dublin stage and Irish nationalism ever since. Indeed, Friel's repeated use of the fictional town of Ballybeg in County Donegal has established the region as a rival to Synge's West as fundamental to the Irish sense of self, while attenuating Donegal from its more historical association with Ulster identity.

The traditional reading of Friel's relationship to Irish nationalism ignores his less successful work of the early 1960s in which he seemed poised to continue the more conventional Realist tradition of such Ulster playwrights as George Shiels and Joseph Tomelty, who wrote plays set in small Northern towns on either side of the border. Such critical amnesia in part derives from the playwright's own decision to withdraw his early plays set in Northern Ireland. While Friel authored thirteen works for the stage, radio, and television from 1958 through 1970, only five plays are currently in print, and of them only one, the immensely popular *Lovers* (1967) is set in Northern Ireland.

A full survey of Friel's eight withdrawn plays of the 1960s for television, radio, and the stage has not been attempted since Ulf Dantanus's comprehensive treatment of 1989, and future scholars would find the task especially daunting because of the general unavailability of these works. While the National Library of Ireland houses Friel's collected papers — containing one-hundred-thirty boxes

of manuscripts, correspondence, contracts, and diverse production ephemera —
the Friel Papers focus overwhelmingly on the stage plays. In other words, the
documents that would allow scholars to reconstruct a comprehensive assessment
of his early career are absent: his *Irish Press* articles, screen plays, essays, and
much of the ancillary material for his minor works. Such a survey is beyond the
scope of this essay as well; however, my intention is to consider Friel's earliest
plays within the context of the Ulster theatre tradition and, specifically, to argue
for the importance of *The Blind Mice* for a new understanding of Friel's early
career.

    Friel started his career as playwright with two radio plays, which were
both broadcast by the BBC Northern Ireland Service in early 1958: *A Sort of
Freedom* on 16 January and *To This Hard House* on 24 April. While the family
dynamics and especially the similar portrayals of self-centred fathers attracted
critical attention in books by D.E.S Maxwell (1973), Ulf Dantanus (1989), and
Elmer Andrews (1992), for the purposes of this exposition it is important to note
that both plays are set in Northern Ireland: the former in Friel's home city of
Derry, and the latter in the fictional village of Meenbanid, which the play locates
outside the actual Mid-Ulster town of Newtownabbey. Although such critics as
Andrews have noted a similar 'personal inflexibility' of both central male
characters, Daniel Frazer and Jack Stone, that makes them especially difficult
fathers or husbands,[2] the plays present quite divergent views of life in Northern
Ireland. While the action of the first play, *A Sort of Freedom*, transpires against
the background of the Frazers' failed attempt to nurture their recently adopted
baby boy, the play quickly focuses on the struggle of two men against labour union
activity in Daniel Frazer's haulage company. At first, both Frazer and his loyal
driver Joe Reddin resist the union's attempt to close the business to non-union
workers, though Frazer eventually fires Reddin to avoid a threatened work
stoppage. *To This Hard House* moves from urban Derry to the village of
Meenbanid, and from a couple seeking to adopt children to a couple with children
old enough to be either married or well into their careers. However, in this play
as well, the central tension concerns the father's attempt to resist social change,
in this case the replacement of Stone's village school with a modern one with
'swimming pool, milk-bar and [...] a rest-room for the teachers!'[3]

    The critical impulse has been to read both plays within the context of
Friel's future career, to see, for example, Jack Frazer as a prototype for the
domineering fathers in such later plays as *Crystal and Fox* or *Living Quarters*.[4]
Similarly, the agon between father and son schoolmasters in *To This Hard House*
sketches out the dynamic that will be developed with greater nuance in Hugh and
Manus O'Donnell of *Translations*. While such a strategic reading of these minor
works allows us to recognize nascent elements that were to become trademarks
of the mature playwright, it ignores the young Friel's relationship to an Ulster
theatre that was thriving in Belfast. Throughout the mid to late 1950s, articles in
*The Belfast Telegraph* frequently discussed aspects of a recognizable tradition of
'Ulster theatre' as characterized by the Ulster Group Theatre and, to a lesser
extent, the Lyric Theatre. Indeed, in the years before the controversy associated
with Sam Thompson's play *Over the Bridge* during the winter of 1959-60, it was

not uncommon for such columnists as Betty Lowery, Jack Loudan, and Dorothy Watters to call for 'a theatre building "worthy of a capital city,"' thus establishing the Group as a Northern counterpart to Dublin's Abbey Theatre.[5] While the Group Theatre could not have claimed to be Ireland's first theatre, during the 1950s it did emerge as the Abbey's genuine rival, for this was a period during which the Abbey, as characterized by Robert Welch, was associated with 'shoddy and often poorly-written formulaic plays'.[6] In fact, during this decade it was not uncommon for such 'Abbey' playwrights as St. John Ervine and Joseph Tomelty to premiere their plays with the Group Theatre, staging them at the Abbey only later.

Within this context of Ulster playwriting, Friel's first play harkens back to the 'social issue' plays of working class Ulster associated with such writers as Cecil Cree, Harry Gibson, and John D. Stewart. Stewart's *Danger, Men Working* (1951), for example, examines labor union tensions at a construction site in Co. Tyrone, and this play was considered important enough to be premiered at London's Lyric Theatre under the direction of Friel's future mentor Tyrone Guthrie. Whereas Sam Thompson's *Over the Bridge*, which premiered in 1960, ignited controversy because it infused the labor union play with sectarian violence, *A Sort of Freedom* produces a more traditionally Ulster play by muting, but not fully erasing, Frazer's association with wealthy Protestant businessmen and Reddin's with working-class Catholicism.

Similarly, *To This Hard House* establishes more than passing links to the works of Patricia O'Connor, one of the Group Theatre's most prolific playwrights. During a career that spanned nearly the entire two decades of the Group's existence, O'Connor authored seven popular plays on diverse aspects of middle-class Ulster life; however, two of her more memorable plays concerned teachers. In her survey of twentieth-century Ulster theatre, Ophelia Byrne recognizes O'Connor's *Highly Efficient* (1942), a play about two rural teachers seeking to reconcile their passion for teaching with enervating state regulations, as one of the most important plays of the 1940s.[7] O'Connor's later play *Master Adams* (1949) stages the retirement of Ballybeg's village schoolmaster as a sentimental narrative in which former students unexpectedly arrange to provide their old mentor with a quaint cottage for his retirement and crucial medical treatment for his daughter.[8] While Friel's radio play fails to share O'Connor's celebration of rural teaching despite its privations, both Friel and O'Connor portray a profession in the midst of painful modernization forced upon traditional rural schools by government bureaucrats.

If neither *A Sort of Freedom* nor *To This Hard House* betrays the direct influence of specific Group Theatre plays, they do establish an overall compatibility with the company's themes that were again manifested in Friel's first stage play, *A Doubtful Paradise* (1960), which the Group staged in August 1960. The Friel Papers contain a letter from Ronald Mason establishing that Friel had submitted the play to the Group in early 1958, and Mason describes it as 'a good Ulster comedy.' Indeed, light comedies set in the North with improbable dilemmas and superficial expositions were as popular in Ulster as their Irish counterparts were in the South. Several Group plays of this era received reviews that lightly chided the company for staging plays filled with 'whimsy' or 'many a shenanigan,' and Friel's comedy about a Derry postal worker enamored with French culture is no more improbable than such Everyman comedies as Joseph Tomelty's *April in Assagh* (1954) or St. John Ervine's *My Brother Tom* (1952).

The Blind Mice occupies a unique place even among Friel's unsanctioned work. While *The Mundy Scheme* (1969), his political satire on the economic intersection of necro-tourism and underdevelopment in the Taoiseach's office, shares the distinction of being the only other full-length stage play to have been withdrawn after its production, it remains available in both a 1969 edition, published jointly with *Crystal and Fox*, and in a Samuel French acting edition that had been altered for American audiences. Moreover, *The Mundy Scheme* enjoyed a partial rehabilitation during Dublin's Friel Festival in 1999, when the play was given a dramatic reading at the Peacock Theatre. Conversely, *The Blind Mice* has never been published, nor has it been revived since its production at the Lyric Theatre the year following its premiere at the Eblana Theatre in 1963. Nevertheless, not only was it his most successful play before *Philadelphia, Here I Come!* (1964), decidedly more popular than *The Enemy Within* (1962), but it marks a considerable advance over his two earlier theatre pieces in his sense of staging.

By the time Friel finished *The Blind Mice* (1963), the playwright had few options for staging it: by 1961 James Young had reorganized the Group Theatre into a company for staging crowd-pleasing extravaganzas, the Lyric Theatre specialized in classics of Europe and the Irish Renaissance, and the Abbey Theatre had rejected the script, even though it had staged *The Enemy Within* during the summer festival of 1962. In an interview with Sean Ward for *The Irish Press* in December 1962, Friel admitted, 'I don't remember exactly what they said about it, but they turned it down flat'.[9] Thus, his agreement with Phyllis Ryan to have her Orion Theatre premiere the play in Dublin can be seen to reflect a decision dictated as much by necessity as the attraction of a Dublin premiere.

This Orion production opened barely a week before the Abbey's revival of Tomelty's *Is the Priest at Home?* and this coincidental staging in Dublin of priest plays by two Northern playwrights speaks to the popularity of clerical plays not just for Dublin audiences, but to the Ulster theatre tradition as well. Tomelty's study of Father Malan's attempts to minister to the diverse social and psychological needs of his church in 'the small town of Marlfield, in Northern Ireland' was premiered by the Group Theatre in May 1954 and remained one of its most popular plays throughout the decade. Indeed, within three years the Group had selected *Is the Priest* for its tours to both Catholic Cork and Anglican Colchester. Along with this priest play, the Group had also staged several about Anglican ministers, including Patricia O'Connor's *Select Vestry* (1945) and Joan Sadler's *The Mustard Seed* (1957), as well as many more that included significant roles for priests or ministers. Moreover, Friel's play about a flawed priest subjected to clerical review premiered barely four years after Patricia O'Connor's *The Sparrow Falls* (1959), a very well-reviewed play that ran at the Group Theatre for over five weeks, and which explores a priest's failure to resolve a venomous rivalry between a Catholic teacher and a strong-willed mother who was a recent convert from the Protestant community. The influence of these Northern portrayals of Catholicism by Tomelty and O'Connor upon Friel are nowhere more apparent than in the scenes of Catholic boycotting against Catholic merchants that is common to all three dramas.

While as early as 1965 Friel had dismissed *The Blind Mice* as 'a bad play',[10] it had been both a successful and admired work since its premiere on 19 February 1963 at Phyllis Ryan's Orion Theatre. Not only did this initial production run for six weeks and more than two dozen performances until the end of March 1963, but Belfast's Lyric Theatre also staged the play the following year. Moreover, within a year of its debut it was to be adapted for the radio by the BBC Home Service of Northern Ireland in November 1963, followed by Radio Éireann in February 1965; in less than five years it was aired on the radio at least six times. While this success with audiences distinguished *The Blind Mice* from the relative failure of Friel's first play, the reviews for both the Dublin and Belfast productions were also quite favourable. Not only did *The Irish Times* praise Friel for the play's intensity and its 'beautifully drawn' characters, but it used the production of the play by Orion to express 'shame for Mr. Ernest Blythe's *nouveau* Abbey Theatre' for having rejected the play.[11] Similarly, the critic for *The Times* praises both the writing and acting of the Belfast production and even expresses his appreciation that 'fortunately for Ireland [Friel] gave up a safe school-mastering job to devote himself to writing'.[12]

Compared to Friel's second play, *The Enemy Within*, which is the first work of his sanctioned canon, *The Blind Mice* stands out. *The Enemy Within* was debuted on 6 August 1962 by the Abbey Theatre as part of its Summer Festival offerings, but even though it had been warmly received by the critic of *The Irish Times* as a 'beautiful character sketch,' the play's run ended before its tenth performance.[13] Nonetheless, this was Friel's first play that could genuinely be described as a success: it was staged by the Lyric Theatre within the year, broadcast once on Radio Éireann in April 1963, and twice that year in Northern Ireland by the BBC Home Service; unlike *The Blind Mice*, however, these radio productions were not subsequently rebroadcast in the following years. In other words, after the quiet failure of *A Doubtful Paradise* two years earlier in Belfast, *The Enemy Within* introduced Friel to a wider audience through its stage and radio productions in the Republic and Northern Ireland. In fact, in his first interview in December 1962 Friel himself encourages such a view of his career's development when he identifies *The Blind Mice* 'as much better than his first work, *The Enemy Within*'.[14]

Curiously, in an interview with Peter Lennon that was published during the Belfast production of *The Blind Mice* in October 1964, Friel expresses his first criticism of what he now calls a 'very poor' play: 'It was too solemn, too intense; I wanted to hit at too many things'.[15] While Thomas Kilroy seeks to draw a qualitative distinction between *The Blind Mice*, which Friel never allowed to be published, and *The Enemy Within*, the first play of his sanctioned canon, most critics who have examined the two more frequently discuss the plays' shared weaknesses of development and staging. Similarly, in the wake of his successes of the later 1960s, Friel himself tended to distance himself from both plays. If *The Blind Mice* is 'a bad play,' *The Enemy Within* is only marginally better: 'There's nothing very wrong with it and there's certainly nothing very good about it'.[16] Within this context, it is telling that while Friel's other plays of the 1960s were published to coincide with their premiers, he did not allow *The Enemy Within* to be published until 1979, more than fifteen years after its initial production.

Although Dantanus posits that Friel's rejection of *The Blind Mice* is 'more emotional and personal than critical,'[17] the play's critical reception has generally followed Friel's dismissal of the play. After citing Friel's own judgment that it is 'a bad play,' D.E.S. Maxwell curtly confirms that '*The Blind Mice* is open to criticism';[18] similarly, Elmer Andrews reassures his readers that the work is 'no more promising than the early radio plays'.[19] Richard Pine agrees that '*The Blind Mice* was a mistake,' yet he develops the most textually sensitive analysis of the play's theme of betrayal both within the family and religion.[20] Ultimately, though, all the previous analyses are based upon the radio version of the play, which cut the ninety-minute stage version down to fifty minutes; however, the stage play proved to be quite popular with audiences in Dublin as well as Belfast and deserves consideration in its own right. Until the script for the stage version was deposited in the Friel Papers, only the much shorter radio script had been available, which is itself absent from the Friel archive.

Comparing Friel's early play-scripts reveals much concerning his evolution as a playwright during this period when he first explored making the transition from fiction to theatre through radio. Friel himself identified that his reason for turning to drama had more to do with his inability to escape the influences of such masters of the short story as Sean O'Faolain and Frank O'Connor than any specific calling to the theatre.[21] Indeed, in 'Self Portrait' he implies that he made this decision around 1960, though he had no substantive stage experience: 'I found myself at the age of thirty [...] almost totally ignorant of the mechanics of play-writing and play-production'.[22] Not surprising, Friel's first stage play, *A Doubtful Paradise*, demonstrates just how difficult it was for the young writer to adapt his skills to the stage.

Being the first work that Friel wrote for the stage, *A Doubtful Paradise* also presents a playwright who sometimes has trouble staging action. Such theorist practitioners as Gay McAuley distinguish two forms of 'extra-dialogic directions' that are differentiated by their position in the play's act-scene structure: the regulatory, which indicate 'the characters' entrances and exits,' and business action 'within the presentational space,' which envision action within a scene.[23] McAuley notes that some writers like Beckett provide comprehensively strict directions, while others leave considerable discretionary freedom to directors or actors to map the script's action; however, his work is not concerned with establishing qualitative distinctions within stage directions that are the subject of this discussion of Friel's plays. Throughout his career, Friel has employed two types of scripted movement for his actors within the presentational space: narrative action, which consists of such simple action to advance the plot as 'Willie rushes at Kevin to silence him,'[24] and emblematic action, where the play's themes are embodied through stylized and often overtly connotative movement. Such plays as *Translations* and *Dancing at Lughnasa* each contain some of the most memorable examples in which the particularity of Friel's directions indicate the scene's importance to the playwright's thematic vision for the work. Friel's emblematic scenes, like the events that culminate in Philly's savage assault on Shane in *The Gentle Island*[25] or the 'near-hysteria' of the sisters' dance in *Dancing at Lughnasa*,[26] are carefully scripted set pieces that embody a play's ethos in a manner that often resists reductive characterization as merely spatial movement.

As a transitional play from the aural medium of radio to the diverse media involved with the stage, *A Doubtful Paradise* only intermittently directs the actors through the stage's space. While Acts 1 and 2 are introduced with considerable regulatory details regarding the set and the initial actions of characters, there is relatively sparse direction during the scenes. Indeed, it is not uncommon for an entire page or two to only note the speaker's intonation without any suggested movement; for example, characters may speak to reflect that they are 'faintly mocking' (*DP*, 6) or 'Quoting' (*DP*, 35) without additional direction. Moreover, twice the young playwright provides only the most ambiguous directions, which are not clearly spoken or gestural, expressed by '?' as in the following:

Gerald   They're gone to the Majestic to a banquet in honour
              of a .......... a commercial
Kevin   ?
Gerald   He's a Frenchman.
Kevin   A French commercial traveller. Sounds like the
              beginning of a dirty joke. (*DP*, 14)[27]

Of course, much of the play contains straightforwardly presentational direction, as when Willie's daughter Chris 'begins to back towards the door' (*DP*, 27) or 'Willie rises from his chair' (*DP*, 44). Thus, though at times the play may lack explicit stage directions, it generally provides reliable and naturalistic ones. However, while the reviewers noted the weak characterization of the main character Willie Logue, the play also betrays its inability to articulate the action of emblematic scenes. For example, consider the celebratory moment early in the play between father and daughter after her first entrance where she announces that Willie's poem has been published in the evening paper:

Chris rushes to her father and kisses him. After she kisses
him they separate and as if they had rehearsed it, they go
through a little pantomime together. They stand facing one
another, about three yards apart, click heels and bow low to
one another. They think they are doing a sort of froggy,
Frenchy mime. (*DP*, 8)

Not long after this scene, Willie admits to his boarder Gerald that he is a Francophile, though the play makes clear that his grasp of the French language and its culture is both shallow and caricaturized (*DP*, 10). Indeed, even before Willie makes his first appearance in the play, he is heard singing 'Frere Jacques' in the hall with a poor accent (*DP*, 4). Thus, the point in the above scene between

Willie and his daughter is not that they share a debased, 'froggy' conception of Frenchness — indeed, the play is about the damage done to his family by his immaturity, which is both cultural and emotional — but that this scene emblematizes his Francophilia only through a brief and generic bow between father and daughter.

Nowhere can Friel's rapid development as a playwright be seen better than when he next presents to his audience a character's pantomime. In *The Blind Mice*, John Carroll, the younger brother of the play's central figure Father Chris Carroll, 'gets to his feet and pantomimes the arrival of Father Rooney' for his mother.[28] Whereas in the case of the earlier play, the 'Frenchy mime' consists of a single action, which defines Frenchness in only the most speculative manner, John Carroll's mime is both more extended and mimetically pertinent to the play's context:

> John:  (*Horribly mincing*) I'm not intruding, am I? Mrs.
>        Carroll, how <u>are</u> you? It's very kind of you to have
>        me to tea. And little John! My, but we're growing
>        into quite a big man, aren't we!
> Lily:  (*Laughing involuntarily*) Aw, quit it, John ...
>        quit it ...
> John:  A little sherry? Well, if you insist — (*As if he
>        were watching a drink being poured*) Ah, ah, just a
>        little — carry on — carry on — yes — a drop
>        more ... (*Satisfied*) Now!

Clearly in this example, there is comprehensive action: not only does John have three distinct stage directions, the second of which is given considerable specificity, but his dialogue indicates both intonation and timing.

Such subtlety in scripted action characterizes the play as a whole; not only does Friel more frequently include narrative action as stage directions, but the play more patiently presents emblematic action. For example, when Willie Logue is introduced in *A Doubtful Paradise*, we are told that he is singing, but little more; rather the play emphasizes only the impression the character should give, but not how to act it. For example, we are told 'the first impression [...] is that he is a happy man; pompous, perhaps and a fool,' but not how the actor is to convey all this; similarly, we are only told that his 'tremendous gusto [is] infectious' (*DP*, 4). In short, while his character's one-hundred and fifty word introduction explains his beliefs and attitudes, it contains not a single stage direction. Conversely, when Chris Carroll first appears in *The Blind Mice*, his introduction is barely ten words longer, but it solely concerns his appearance and movements (*BM*, 24-5). Friel describes Chris' hair, each article of his clothing (jacket, shirt, and trousers), and several minutes of action:

> He paces the length of the stage and then the breadth,
> counting the steps to himself. Then he stops beside the fire.
> He sees the photograph of himself above the mantlepiece and

> examines it. His movements are jerky, unsteady: He might be
> discovering movement for the first time. He then takes a seat
> — preferably a diningroom chair, upright, comfortless. (*BM*, 25)

There is no single, dominant emblematic scene in *Philadelphia, Here I Come!*; however, whether one considers Gar's performance of Mendelssohn's concerto,[29] or the forced rambunctiousness of the lads who arrive to give Gar his send off,(*SP*, 69-71), one recognizes the impact of Guthrie's staging practice on the playwright. Indeed, in *Philadelphia*, Friel masterfully juxtaposes youthful histrionics, in which 'Tranquility is [the] enemy' (*SP*, 69), to the elder characters' more finely modulated actions, as when S.B. casually 'removes his teeth' without fanfare (*SP*, 48). In comparison to Friel's newly acquired, skillful staging in this play, the emblematic scenes in *The Enemy Within* and *The Blind Mice* appear contrived and almost Victorian in the rigidity of their application of tableau principles. In the first play, two related scenes are generally discussed as of emblematic importance to the play's interpretation: Columba's struggle to decide whether to accompany the messenger Brian into battle[30] and the final act's reprise of this earlier scene when he is confronted by his brother Eoghan (*EW*, 62-9).[31] The first, which has been seen as fundamental to the dominant critical interpretation of the play as staging Columba's struggle between the religious and the temporal, achieves its climax by stiffly positioning Columba between Brian, who represents temporal politics, and Grillaan, the monk's spiritual confessor; indeed, the script didactically includes that 'he is torn between the two' (*EW*, 33). By comparison, the interrogation scene in *The Blind Mice* is the early Friel's most visually elaborate: the young priest is '[shoved] roughly back into a seat,' ambient lighting entirely cut to a spotlight 'focused directly on his face,' and his four accusers surround him to rapidly fire off more than two dozen comments and denunciations (*BM*, 52-3). This scene stages a more complex moment than its analogous temptation scene in *The Enemy Within*; however, the playwright's keener attention to lighting, character placement, and narrative development is employed for a scene of melodramatic reductiveness at least equal to that in *The Enemy Within*.

Ultimately, several scenes of *The Blind Mice* can be criticized for their sentimentality, as is the case with the two scenes in which the psychologically traumatized young priest sings 'Three Blind Mice' (*BM*, 54 & 85). However, this play is more significant for its introduction of a set piece that will become important to such plays as *Aristocrats* (1979), *Dancing at Lughnasa* (1990), and *Give Me Your Answer, Do!* (1997): the casual aftermath to the family's communal dinner (*BM*, 63-72).[32] If other scenes are too focused on the debate between act and spiritual intention (*BM*, 38-46, 73-5), the younger brother's envy of the family's longstanding favouritism shown to Chris (*BM*, 57-61), and the hypocrisy of Northern Ireland's Catholics (*BM*, 11-12, 48-51, 55-6), this episode provides the first example of the young playwright's ability to write a naturalistic ensemble scene (*BM*, 63-72). As family and friends sit slowly drinking tea and discussing plans amid snippets of local news, Friel demonstrates his ability to delineate familial relations that will later attract comparisons to Chekhov. Moreover, this example is additionally noteworthy for the scene's emphasis on the matriarch, Lily Carroll, who uses this scene to initiate the rehabilitation of her priest son. Decades before Friel becomes recognized as a writer of the Irish female experience, Lily is the first of his fully developed women. Indeed, she is one of Friel's rare matriarchs and the only character before Chris Mundy of *Dancing at Lughnasa* whose importance eclipses that of the play's father, in this case Arthur Carroll. She has the stage at the work's beginning and ending, and throughout the drama she plays a major role in managing her three adult children. Conversely, Arthur Carroll is Friel's most comic and benign father, who spends most of the play in the family's shop, often appearing only momentarily, when 'he sticks his head round' the door (*BM*, 6, 7, 15, 23, 32, 48). Indeed, it is interesting to note that in Friel's first attempt to shift his focus to the generation born after the formation of the Irish state, he employs the mother to blunt the psychological impact of the patriarchal father which is so potent in such plays as *Philadelphia*, *The Mundy Scheme*, and *Aristocrats*.

Less than four months after the premiere of *Philadelphia, Here I Come!* an article by Jonathan North in *Ulster Week* set out to assess Ulster's 'Big Five' playwrights. North claims that while Friel had recently caught the attention of international audiences, *Over the Bridge* by Sam Thompson may be the best recent play by any Ulsterman; yet, he suspects that John Hamilton 'may yet be the biggest success' of them all.[33] In fact, even in the wake of Friel's successes with *The Blind Mice* and *Philadelphia*, the article suggests that his work may be the most flawed: 'his plays set out problems which they make no attempt to solve'.[34] It is instructive to return to North's article, to that moment in January 1965, for it reminds us that before Friel was recognized as the pre-eminent Irish playwright of the postwar era, he was considered one of Ulster's many aspiring playwrights and a peer of the younger Angry Stewart Love and the older Social Realist Sam Thompson. Indeed, if one considers also Friel's radio plays of 1958, only the last of his first six plays is set in the Republic, while four are set in Northern Ireland — two in Derry, and the others in Meenbanid or Thian Hee.[35] In other words, as noted by the *Irish Times* review of *The Blind Mice*, despite being a nationalist and a Catholic, Friel was more a Northern Irish playwright in the tradition of Joseph Tomelty than a Southern Irish one: 'His characters are real — but [...] they may be more real for Northern Irish Catholics than anybody else'.[36]

With its focus on Friel's plays of the early 1960s, this article has sought to trace the playwright's development, not the providential one of his published canon, but the more intricate one of his extant radio and stage plays. In order to become the author of *Philadelphia, Here I Come!*, as well as his subsequent innovative plays, Friel had to do more than change the imagined locus of his work to the Republic, he had to accomplish a comprehensive renovation in his dramaturgy — not merely of the way he conceptualized narrative, but of the manner in which he envisioned action upon the stage. In this effort to understand the young playwright's evolution, *The Blind Mice* must become a more widely discussed work, and not one blithely dismissed as 'a bad play.'

## NOTES

[1] Brian Friel 'Brian Friel's Lenten Diary', *The Irish Press*, 9 March 1963, p. 8.

[2] Elmer Andrews, *The Art of Brian Friel: Neither Reality nor Dreams* (New York: St. Martin's Press, 1995), p. 46.

[3] All references to *To This Hard House* are to the playscript contained in the Friel Papers, National Library of Ireland, manuscript #37,140/1.

[4] Richard Pine, *The Diviner: The Art of Brian Friel* (Dublin: University College Dublin Press, 1999), pp. 99-100.

[5] Dorothy Watters, 'The Group's Contribution to Ulster Theatre', *Belfast Telegraph*, 5 March 1955, p. 4.

[6] Robert Welch, *The Abbey Theatre 1899-1999: Form and Pressure* (Oxford: Oxford University Press, 1999), p.162.

[7] Ophelia Byrne, *State of Play: The Theatre and Cultural Identity in 20th Century Ulster* (Belfast: The Linen Hall Library, 2001), p. 35.

[8] *Master Adams* premiered in November 1949, during the period that Friel lived in Belfast to complete his teacher training at St. Joseph's College, see Ulf Dantanus, *Brian Friel: A Study* (London: Faber & Faber, 1988), p. 35. While it is tempting to speculate that Friel may have seen this play and thus adopted O'Connor's 'Ballybeg,' Co. Antrim, for his fictional town in Co. Donegal, Friel himself noted in a private letter to the author that he does not recall seeing even one play during his year in Belfast.

[9] Sean Ward, 'Test for Abbey Rejects', *Irish Press*, 10 December, 1962, p. 8.

[10] Paul Delaney (ed.), *Brian Friel in Conversation* (Ann Arbor: University of Michigan Press, 2000), p. 28.

[11] 'The Blind Mice' at the Eblana', *Irish Times*, 20 February 1963, p. 4.

[12] 'Early Plays by Brian Friel', *The Times*, 7 October 1964, p. 13.

[13] 'Friel's Great Play of Ulster's Hero-Saint', *Irish Times*, 7 August 1962, p. 10.

[14] Ward, 'Test for Abbey Rejects'.

[15] Christopher Murray (ed.), *Brian Friel: Essays, Diaries, Interviews: 1964-1999.* (London: Faber and Faber, 1999), p. 20.

[16] Ibid, p. 8

[17] *Brian Friel: A Study*, p. 68.

[18] D.E.S. Maxwell, *Brian Friel* (Lewisburg, Penn: Bucknell University Press, 1973), p. 54.

[19] *The Art of Brian Friel: Neither Reality nor Dreams*, p. 55.

[20] *The Diviner: The Art of Brian Friel*, p. 106-7.

[21] Delaney, *Brian Friel in Conversation*, p. 171.

[22] *Brian Friel: Essays, Diaries, Interviews: 1964-1999.* pp. 41-2

[23] Gay Macauley, *Space in Performance: Making Meaning in the Theatre* (Ann Arbor: University of Michigan Press, 2000), p. 224.

[24] Brian Friel, *A Doubtful Paradise*, p. 31. All references to this text are to the playscript contained in the Friel Papers, National Library of Ireland, manuscript #37,043/1. Henceforth referred to in parentheses, as *DP*

[25] Brian Friel, *The Gentle Island* (Loughcrew: The Gallery Press, 1993), pp. 43-5.

[26] Brian Friel, *Dancing at Lughnasa*, (London: Faber & Faber, 1990), pp. 22.

[27] The other example pertains to the character Maggie, Willie's wife, on page 37 of the manuscript.

[28] Brian Friel, *The Blind Mice*, p. 8. All references to this text are to the playscript contained in the Friel Papers, National Library of Ireland, manuscript #37,046/1. Henceforth referred to in parentheses as *BM*.

[29] Brian Friel, *Selected Plays* (Washington, DC: The Catholic University Press, 1986), p. 36. Henceforth referred to in parentheses as *SP*

[30] Brian Friel, *The Enemy Within* (Newark, Delaware: The Proscenium Press, 1979), p. 27-33. Henceforth referred to in parentheses as *EW*.

[31] See, for example, Andrews pp. 79-80, Dantanus pp. 80-1, F.C. McGrath, *Brian Friel's (Post)Colonial Drama: Language, Illusion, and Politics* (Syracuse: Syracuse University Press, 1999). p. 68, and Richard Allen Cave, 'Friel's dramaturgy: the visual element,' *The Cambridge Companion to Brian Friel* (ed. Anthony Roche). Cambridge: Cambridge University Press, 2006. 129-41. p. 132.

[32] Tom Breslin, the play's union organizer who hopes to marry into this 'highly thought of' family (*BM* ii), provides the most direct link to *Aristocrats* through his similarity to Eamon.

[33] Jonathan North, 'The "Big Five" of Irish Drama', *Ulster Week*. 6 January 1965, pp. 3 & 8.

[34] Ibid.

[35] Meenbanid, the fictional site of the Stone family's home in *To This Hard House*, is described as a town neighbouring Newtownabbey, which is seven miles north of Belfast. The site of Thian Hee in *The Blind Mice* is less certain; however, at one point Arthur Carroll laments that because of their residence in Northern Ireland, his business' insurance policy does not cover the vandalism done by rock throwers: 'there's a wee footnote to my insurance: All riots, it says, except in Northern Ireland!' (*BM*, p. 19).

[36] 'The Blind Mice' at the Eblana', *Irish Times*. 20 February 1963, p. 4.

SCOTT BOLTWOOD *is Associate Professor of English at Emory & Henry College, Virginia. He has been a Visiting Professor at University of Ulster, Northern Ireland, and a Research Fellow at the Academy of Irish Cultural Heritages in Londonderry. His work on Irish playwrights such as Brian Friel, Augusta Gregory, Frank McGuinness, and Dion Boucicault has appeared in journals including* Irish Studies Review *and* Modern Drama. *His monograph* Brian Friel, Ireland, and The North *was published by Cambridge University Press in 2007.*

Irish Theatre International, Vol. 2, No. 1, pp. 16-27

# Brian Friel, Tyrone Guthrie and Thornton Wilder

CHRISTOPHER MURRAY

*In the congruence of like minds Brian Friel educated himself in the best modern theatrical production values by looking for models to Tyrone Guthrie and Thornton Wilder at the same time. And yet we have to accept that Friel was always his own man. As playwright he did not entirely share Wilder's sunny disposition, his insistence that even in the midst of death we are in life, even if only by the skin of our teeth. Friel's ironic take on life is darker, more pessimistic, and truer to the Irish — to say Celtic — sensibility. And so, in spite of Guthrie's hearty endorsement Friel was by no means a slavish imitator. When all is said, Friel is closer to Chekhov in temperament and style. But Friel is Protean. His inspiration derives from multiple influences quietly internalised and transformed. Guthrie helped enormously to channel these early influences, which included the work of Wilder, and thus to enable his protégé develop his genius for the stage. This article defines a triangular relationship between the dramaturgy of Friel, Guthrie and Wilde within which Friel's stagecraft might be looked at anew.*

If aficionados of Brian Friel's plays and stagecraft were to see the following quotations in print I believe they would have no doubt of the authorship of each, even if they might hesitate about the dating of each:

> It is often said that today's theatre is a director's theatre. Hardly less often a supplementary statement follows: that the modern director has got above his [*sic*] station, is too big for his [*sic*] boots. It is true that the director of a play now draws more attention than used to be the case. I suppose when it became apparent that in the movies the director was the dominant influence [...] it was then that public and critics began to wonder whether in the theatre this creature might not exert a certain influence.

And the other quotation:

> Each individual's assertion to an absolute reality can only be inner, very inner. And here the method of staging finds its justification. [...] Our claim, our hope, our despair are in the mind — not in things, not in "scenery". Molière said that for the theatre all he needed was a platform and a passion or two. [...] One way to shake off the nonsense of the nineteenth-century staging is to make fun of it. This play parodies the stock-company plays I used to see [...] when I was a boy. [...] I am not an innovator but a rediscoverer of forgotten goods.

Neither quotation is, in fact, from Friel although each echoes views voiced by Friel in interviews as late as 1990 and the essay 'The Theatre of Hope and Despair'. The first is actually from Tyrone Guthrie,[1] the second from Thornton Wilder's preface to his plays.[2] Their introduction here allows me to define a triangular relationship — Friel, Guthrie, Wilder — within which Friel's stagecraft might be looked at anew.

As is widely known, for six months in the year 1963 Brian Friel studied — the word is not too strong — under Tyrone Guthrie at the latter's new theatre then opening in Minneapolis. Up to this point Friel had some little experience as a playwright, though his first work, *A Sort of Freedom* and *To This Hard House*, took the form of radio plays broadcast by BBC Northern Ireland in 1958. As has been said, 'Friel wrote these plays while he was primarily occupied with the short story,'[3] and before he had any real knowledge of the stage. He himself has dismissed his first stage play, *A Doubtful Paradise*, premiered by the Group Theatre in Belfast in 1959, and of the plays staged before the Minneapolis adventure leaves for consideration only *The Enemy Within* (1962). This play was directed by Ria Mooney for the Abbey Theatre then playing at the Queen's. She was worried about its understated qualities and suggested in a letter to Friel that he provide stronger curtain lines. He didn't know what she was talking about: 'As you will probably have guessed my knowledge of the business of theatre is minimal. I don't believe I would know a strong curtain line if I saw one.'[4] He suggested that Ria supply the curtain lines herself but promised to get to rehearsal two days before the opening on 6 August. Small wonder that he later described himself at this point as 'almost totally ignorant of the mechanics of play-writing and play-production apart from an intuitive knowledge. Like a painter who has never studied anatomy; like a composer with no training in harmony.' *The Blind Mice* (Eblana 1963), which opened just before Friel left Ireland, was old-fashioned realism, and remains unpublished. Consequently, his sojourn in Minneapolis was 'an important period in a practical way. I learned about the physical elements of plays, how they are designed, built, landscaped. I learned how actors thought, how they approached a text, their various ways of trying to realise it.'[5] Later, in interview with Mel Gussow, Friel was to put this a little differently: 'The experience was enabling to the extent that it gave me courage and daring to attempt things.'[6] On his return to Ireland he was able to complete the first script of *Philadelphia, Here I Come!* by early September 1963[7] with unwonted speed. He sent Guthrie the script for comment, and eventually super-scribed on Guthrie's enthusiastic letter dated 7 October 1963, 'I carried out all his suggestions.'[8] Guthrie then recommended the play enthusiastically to Friel's agent at Curtis Brown and would have directed the premiere himself were he not tied up through 1964. Later he offered detailed criticisms of Hilton Edwards's production, which must have proved useful 'notes' for the Broadway premiere.[9]

\*\*\*

I surmise that Friel began writing *Philadelphia* while in Minneapolis, the loneliness before his family joined him perhaps inspiring the feeling in that play. Otherwise, he spent his days at the Guthrie Theatre attending rehearsals as both 'observer' and 'apprentice' (his terms).[10] Rehearsals started on 11 March 1963,[11] Friel observing Guthrie directing *Hamlet* (opened 7 May 1963), *The Miser* (opened 8 May), *Three Sisters* (opened 18 June) and *Death of a Salesman* (opened 16 July). These were the four shows Guthrie directed in his first year in Minneapolis. Friel names only the first three in the interview with Gussow, but it is hard to believe he had not had access to Guthrie's thoughts also on the staging of *Salesman* when one opens the first page of the published text of *Philadelphia, Here I Come!* (Faber, 1965) to find a tripartite setting of kitchen bedroom and forestage or 'apron' which is a neutral area to be used for scenes from the past. Whatever about that, Friel sat in on rehearsals of the other three productions and presumably discussed aspects of them with Guthrie.[12] *Hamlet* on a bare stage newly designed by Tanya Moiseiwisch must have been particularly fascinating to a young writer who took Abbey realism as his touchstone. Richard Cave claims that 'what Friel registered in Minneapolis as "innovative and visually exciting" were just this sensitive spatial awareness and its function within Guthrie's style of directing.'[13] Cave is here contesting director Joe Dowling's earlier statement that 'in spite of his early apprenticeship with Tyrone Guthrie [...] Friel never really developed a sense of the possibilities of stage design as a way of expressing the imagery of his plays.' Cave maintains that Dowling misses the point by speaking of stage *design* instead of scenography. I'm not so sure. What Dowling means, I think, is illustrated by his claim that in the love scene in *Translations* Friel's stage direction shows his 'lack of concern for the visual environment'.[14] The stage direction in question reads: '*This scene* [2.2] *may be played in the schoolroom, but it would be preferable to lose—by lighting—as much of the schoolroom as possible, and to play the scene in a vaguely "outside" area.*'[15] How do we register the phrase 'vaguely outside'? As indeterminate? Yet in the text both lovers refer to the wet grass beneath their feet. It cannot be an interior setting. Dowling is right. Friel learned from Guthrie that a writer can leave a lot to the audience's imagination. A director is there to ensure that the audience sees via the actors' performance what the imagination ought to apprehend, in action, mood, feeling and meaning.

Cave further charges that in any case whatever Friel registered in Minneapolis occurred 'while observing Guthrie *in the rehearsal room*; and in that situation none of the trappings to do with a set would be present.'[16] I should have thought that Friel observed not just Guthrie but the whole *process* of rehearsal, involving the actors' inhabiting a space meant to represent Hamlet's world, for example, as well as close interpretation of the text, as one can see from actor Alfred Rossi's record of the rehearsals of *Hamlet*. The play-within-the play and the closet scenes, it is clear from Rossi's detailed accounts, were meticulously rehearsed in terms of positioning, how the lighting would work, and how facial expressions would be seen. Guthrie was rehearsing for performance on a bare stage, we should recall. We should also bear in mind that Friel saw not only rehearsals but the finished product at dress rehearsal and surely on opening night also. In his letter to Dowling and the company performing the production of *Philadelphia* at the Guthrie Theatre in 1996, referred to above, Friel emphasised that *Philadelphia* was 'the first thing I wrote in a state of near-giddiness when I came back to Ireland, still on a Guthrie high.' It seems clear he is not referring to jetlag. The merits of *Philadelphia, Here I Come!,* and they include major advances in stagecraft over *The Enemy Within* (1962), are here graciously deferred to his first theatrical master. In Minneapolis, as he says elsewhere, he learned a great deal 'about the iron discipline of theatre.'[17]

Guthrie had a missionary zeal for the concept of theatre as ritual. It is a concept I see as equally prominent in the Friel canon. Accordingly, it may be illuminating to pursue this theme before turning to the third figure in the triangular relationship, Thornton Wilder. Writing of the predecessor to his Minneapolis theatre, the archetypal Shakespeare Theatre in Stratford, Ontario, which opened in 1953, Guthrie emphasised:

> The stage is planned upon the theory that illusion is not the aim of performance. The shape of the auditorium, in which the spectators are constantly and inevitably aware of the presence of other spectators, is a constant reminder that the performance is what it is: a ritual in which actors and spectators are alike taking part. This idea appeals, I think, because it happens to be true; whereas the idea of illusion demands self-deception, demands that you believe that to be "really" happening which is clearly fictitious.[18]

In a later book, published in 1965, he has a chapter headed 'Theatre as Ritual' and I imagine all involved in his rehearsals got an earful of this doctrine. Guthrie saw the history of theatre as a seamless patterned garment which is priestly no matter what specific ritual or set of beliefs it either celebrated or sought to explode. *Oedipus the King* (or *Oedipus Rex*, as he always called it) was his paradigm, and as it was in critical terms for Aristotle in the *Poetics* so it was for Guthrie as director the touchstone of excellence for all tragedy (or its equivalents in modern times). That much is clear from the film which survives of Guthrie's production of *Oedipus* at Stratford, Ontario in 1955. In its formality and ceremoniousness, akin to Japanese Noh, that film embodies Guthrie's ritualistic ideas. In 'Theatre as Ritual' Guthrie assembles a rather ramshackle anthropological argument to bolster his contention that 'theatre relates itself to God by means of ritual. It does so more consciously than any other activity, except prayer, because, like organized prayer, it is the direct descendant of primitive religious ceremonies.'[19] Ritual is thus a specific kind of *mimesis*, a ceremonious re-enactment of a known narrative with a transcendent motive (in contrast, say, to Brecht's *gestus*, with its material or historic purpose).

Friel, then, became in this regard a disciple of Guthrie. Recently, he described him as his 'foster-father'.[20] He is in agreement with Guthrie on the ritualistic basis of all theatre: 'Ritual is part of all drama. Drama without ritual is poetry without rhythm — hence not poetry, not drama. That is not to say that ritual is an "attribute" of drama: it is the essence of drama. Drama is a RITE, and always religious in the purest sense.'[21] I take 'religious' here and in Guthrie to mean 'binding' in the Latin sense (*religere*), whereby the community is through the process of serious drama lifted out of mundane considerations and bound to supernatural ones. It is a basis from which to work, not a doctrine with which to work. As a modernist and a sceptic Friel makes use of ritual to expose the bereft nature of humankind. Indeed, as will appear, his habitual practice in the plays is actually to empty out ritual, and in the cleared-out space, like T.S. Eliot in *Four Quartets,* 'to build a new life of the spirit'.²² In that sense he secularises Guthrie's theory of ritual to a paradoxical degree. Tellingly, Friel has said that when he used *céilí* dance music in *Philadelphia, Here I Come!* and in *Dancing at Lughnasa* 'in both plays the purpose was to explode theatrically the stifling rituals and discretions of family life.'²³

The Frielian critique is constantly of a godless society and provides an indictment of those who might have turned ritual into vital, loving release from loneliness and guilt. A clear example is offered in the ritualistic game of chess in *Philadelphia,* a nightly re-enactment between Gar's natural and spiritual fathers, neither of whom acts to save Gar from his despair: following as it does upon the nightly recitation of the family rosary, which in the 1950s and 1960s thrived under Father Peyton's slogan 'the family that prays together stays together,' the game of checkers appears as moral evasion. This family will not stay together. The bond that might have lent it cohesiveness is allowed to dissolve tragically. Madge's comment, taken by Canon O'Byrne as merely hilarious, is in fact an ironic condemnation of his failure in priestly duty: 'She says *I wait* till the rosary's over and the kettle's on ... hee-hee-hee.'²⁴ Private Gar forces home the point that the Canon's holding back from his responsibility is blasphemous: 'Why don't you speak, then? Prudence, arid Canon? Prudence be damned! Christianity isn't prudent — it's insane!' We have to remind ourselves that though the speaker here is Private Gar, a different actor from Public Gar, it is still Gar O'Donnell, a single human entity, whose consciousness sees through the Canon's complacency and angrily holds him accountable, as we also must, for Gar's situation, more spiritual than economic.

In other plays this visionary consciousness lacks the luxury of ghostly invisible presence. It can be created in the audience's mind through the violent contrast between cold officialdom and vulnerable youth, as in *Winners* (Part 1 of *Lovers,* 1967, a play dedicated to Guthrie 'with great affection and great admiration'), or a visionary consciousness may be vested in some outcast, some 'playboy' figure (in Synge's sense) as Skinner in *The Freedom of the City* (1973) or Keeney in *Volunteers* (1975) or Eamonn in *Aristocrats* (1979). In *Winners,* the two commentators at the inquest of Joe and Mag drily provide data that come nowhere near helping the audience to understand how and why the teenagers at the centre of the play died. Instead the juxtaposition of commentators and young protagonists creates an irony which is powerfully alienating. In more complex ways, *The Freedom of the City* (1973) uses a similar kind of irony to cast the ritual of the official enquiry into disgrace through juxtaposition with representation of the three fully humanised at the heart of the enquiry, who, by Friel's use of double time, are at once dead and within the duration of the play fully alive. The skills in stagecraft controlling this play appear now, years after the second official and interminable enquiry into the actual events of Bloody Sunday which lie behind the play, even more impressive as a Brechtian critique of an unjust and brutally unimaginative society. In this play the governing ritual is a false one: the panoply of British rationalism at work within a judicial theatrical form is undermined by the pattern of prejudice governing the re-enactment of events, given what the audience knows as witness of these events proceeding in parallel time. The irony serves to accuse those who might have saved the young people. Skinner, Friel's centre of consciousness within the play and one of the three sacrificial victims of the tragedy, assumes the role of Lord Mayor in order to confer the freedom of the city on his two fellow-marchers taking refuge in the Guildhall, but Skinner is crucially aware that his action is at once meaningless and ceremonial, a form of anti-theatre. Earlier, entering dressed up in the mayoral robes, he had quoted from *King Lear*: 'You're much deceived; in nothing am I changed / But in my garments,' lines that later on underline the lack of change inherent in his ritualistic conferring of benefits on his fellow-victims dressed as aldermen. The emptiness of Skinner's 'ceremony' (his word, *SP* 136) ironically points to the emptiness of the official ritual in the form of an Enquiry. But before all three leave the mayor's parlour Skinner insists that the ceremonial sword he drove into a painting of the presiding image of this bastion of governance be left there: 'Don't touch that! [...] Allow me my gesture' (*SP* 163). Nothing could be more theatrical. Unless it be the whole of *Living Quarters* (1977), where the ritual of theatre is self-consciously deployed to re-tell the Phaedra story and to reshape it into a rehearsal play with a difference.

In *Volunteers*, where the image of an archaeological dig vies with the image of the beginnings of Dublin's new development in the form of a huge hotel on a Viking site, the excavation suggests the emptying out process referred to above. Disparate cultural references are provided in postmodernist style, old bones, Viking 'trial pieces' if you will, Hamlet the Dane echoed by Keeney and Hamlet's confusion associated with the strong emphasis on something being rotten in the state of the Irish republic. The futile attempt to reconstruct a vase from ancient shards likewise serves to point up the lack of any unifying ritual which might give meaning to the participation of republican prisoners in challenging so-called progress. I recall the puzzled question of the *Irish Times* critic at the time, Seamus Kelly, 'what is your point, Mr. Friel?'[25] It took a poet to point out that the play's title 'has a sacral edge which blunts (nevertheless) to sanctimoniousness, and it is this sanctimoniousness that the play is intent on devastating.'[26]

The history plays, *Translations* (1980) and *Making History* (1988) are by definition ritual offerings, in that a history play re-enacts and invariably poses to the audience the question first posed by the actor playing Cassius at the Globe in 1599 after the conspirators had killed Caesar: 'How many ages hence / Shall this our lofty scene be acted over, / In states unborn, and accents yet unknown?' (3.1.111-13). Modern editors end these lines with an exclamation mark, but the First Folio has a question mark. It was a genuine question in 1599, skilfully posed in balancing past, present and future. The ritual killing is transformed into the ritual of theatre to be re-enacted with every performance in some language or other. Cue *Translations*. There is no assassination on stage, to be sure, but there is a strong sense that Yolland has been executed off by the Donnelly twins. The governing ritual of the play, however, is twofold and oppositional; the mapping of a district involving killing off a language, and the teaching in a traditional hedge school, a daily re-enactment of age-old procedures, also about to be killed off. What is left is no doubt debatable. But once again the myth of progress is held in question, that much seems certain, and for all that Hugh Mór O'Donnell can say the price is likely to be high. I interpret the end of the play ominously. Hugh's stumbling translation of the opening of Virgil's *Aeneid* recording the history leading to the establishment of imperial Rome is, no doubt, a bardic recitation of myth in the sense Guthrie would have approved. But I think of Walter Benjamin's famous comment, 'There is no document of civilization which is not at the same time a document of barbarism.'[27] Thus does Friel 'brush history against the grain.' The same point may be made, *mutatis mutandis*, regarding *Making History*.

Faith Healer (1979) is a brilliant case in favour of interpreting Friel's plays as ritualistic in disturbing but ultimately bountiful ways. Guthrie remarked: 'Artists are ministers. Artists bring healing and knowledge. The theatre is a temple.'[28] Again, this is probably too blunt, too sweeping, to be endorsed by Friel without qualification. Yet in an interview with Fintan O'Toole in 1982 Friel said that *Faith Healer* is 'some kind of metaphor for the art, the craft of writing, or whatever it is. And the great confusion we all have about it, those of us who are involved in it.'[29] It can be said, however, that Guthrie did not 'do' confusion, on which Friel's art lives promise-crammed. In his opening monologue Frank describes the settings in Scotland and Wales where he fetched up on one-night stands healing for a living: 'The kirks or meeting-houses or schools — all identical, all derelict. Maybe in a corner a withered sheaf of wheat from a harvest thanksgiving of years ago or a fragment of a Christmas decoration across a window — relics of abandoned rituals' (*SP* 332). Nicholas Grene makes the point that the question for the interpretation of *Faith Healer* is how Friel 'sees the survival of "relics of abandoned rituals" in the modern period.'[30] That is well said, since the next line Frank speaks is: 'Because the people we moved among were beyond that kind of celebration.' In short, Christian belief, Christian ritual, no longer energises their lives: nor Frank Hardy's life, for that matter. In *Dancing at Lughnasa* (1990) Friel was to go much further in exploring a community bereft in that regard: it is quite clear that the rituals father Jack recalls from his time in Ryanga are infinitely more life-sustaining than the 'relics' of harvest in Ballybeg, where they are associated only with mindless mischief and violence and where they serve to point up once again the failure of the Christian tradition (as in *Philadelphia*) to vitalise and support the spirit of the people.

In *Faith Healer* the matter is more philosophically focused. It may be said that Frank Hardy, in however debased a form, is a Christ figure. In so far as Christ was sometimes in the Middle Ages equated with Julius Caesar, the latter's assassination may be related to the Christian sacrifice, or else, says Brutus, 'were this a savage spectacle' (3.1.223). Frank's death, too, is an assassination, albeit one devoid of any political or, for that matter, any other public meaning. We never hear of the inquest's verdict. It is an interesting omission. It leaves the interpretation of Frank's death mainly dependent on his own closing words in the play, where he invokes iconographically the landscape, the setting, as in a Renaissance painting, of Christ's death. Frank's progress across a yard which turns into two yards, a wooden door leading to the second, is the pilgrim's progress, for in effect Frank is not Christ but an imitation of Christ in a godless age. 'I passed through that [door] and there was the other, the large yard. And I knew it at once' (*SP* 375). The poetry of his description is mystical: 'It was a September morning, just after dawn. The sky was orange and everything glowed with a soft radiance — as if each detail of the scene had its own self-awareness and was satisfied with itself.' He is both within and outside nature, as the homely but threatening farmyard details suggest: the tractor and trailer, in the back of which the four implements, axe, crowbar, mallet and hay-fork await their time, side-by-side with 'two mature birch trees and the wind was sufficient to move them.' 'About suffering they were never wrong, the Old Masters,' said Auden, and we see it here again in Friel, this precise inclusiveness of the banal and the tremendous:

> They never forgot
> That even the dreadful martyrdom must run its course
> Anyhow in a corner, some untidy spot
> Where the dogs go on with their doggy life and the
> torturer's horse
> Scratches its innocent behind on a tree.[31]

Before Frank speaks his final lines and moves slowly downstage, he '*takes off his hat as if he were entering a church and holds it at his chest,*' reinforcing his return to a holy place, here and now Guthrie's 'temple,' which gives Frank 'for the first time [...] a simple and genuine sense of home-coming' (*SP* 376). The audience is taken along in imagination to the whole dramatic point of the play; the sudden darkness ('*quick black*') into which Frank steps. Who can doubt that his death is a release and in a strange sense a triumph? So it was received by the first audience at the Abbey, in Dowling's production in August 1980. Yeats, citing Lady Gregory, said that 'tragedy must be a joy to the man who dies.'[32] Thus Friel's tatterdemalion hero keeps faith with his uncertain tragic destiny and in so doing rediscovers transcendence for a modern audience. *Faith Healer* is exceptional in its hypostatic, sacramental power. Here ritual functions positively and in the literal, liturgical sense 'mysteriously'.

\*\*\*

Friel attended rehearsals of all of the plays which opened during his eleven-week stay at the Guthrie Theatre Minneapolis in 1963. Besides *Hamlet* these included *Three Sisters* and *The Miser*. He would have seen three quite different plays from different periods, with different theatrical styles. I would argue that all three lodged in Friel's mind, to become fertile influences on his own work. *Hamlet*, being Guthrie's signature production, doubtless made the greatest impact, and its ritualism lies *passim* behind Friel's work, as shown above. *Three Sisters* lay dormant for many years but eventually emerged in his choice for the second production of the Field Day Theatre Company in 1981, in Friel's own version of the text. Strangely, he worked on it at the same time as *Translations*, and described it as 'a very important play.'[33] Molière's *The Miser*, in turn, was a great favourite of Guthrie's and he had directed it as a touring production around village halls in north-east England in the 1948-49 season. 'Here again,' he then wrote, 'the convention of the production was an attempt approximately to reproduce the actor-audience relation for which the play was written; and [...] the audience in these villages is not less but more keen and intelligent than the present metropolitan audience, which tends to be over-supplied with entertainment.'[34] Assuming Guthrie chose *The Miser* for similar reasons in Minneapolis, it may be guessed that the general idea stayed with Friel when Field Day toured the small towns of Northern Ireland in 1980. They did not do *The Miser* but they occasionally did farce, specifically *The Communication Cord* (1982) and Mahon's *The School for Wives*, 'after Molière', (1984).

This is where the other side of the triangle in this general argument, Thornton Wilder, comes briefly into view. The second quotation which began this article derives from Wilder's preface to his 1962 Penguin edition of *Three Plays*: 'Each individual's assertion to an absolute reality can only be inner, very inner.' It might be Brian Friel speaking. When in 1970 Des Rushe asked Friel what playwrights he admired he did not hesitate over who came first: 'I admire Thornton Wilder immensely. He is one of the greatest dramatists of our time.'[35] There are the three 'clever' one-act plays, dating from 1931, all of which make use of 'an impersonal Stage Manager as chorus to the joys and sorrows they introduce.'[36] Friel knew and admired these one-acts, but Wilder's best-known play is *Our Town* (1938), set in a small country town called Grover's Corners. It is not too much to say that this rural American town became Hibernicized as Ballybeg; it has been said that act 3 of *Our Town* 'may well have been a precedent for Friel' in the writing of *Dancing at Lughnasa*[37] but the kinship goes further than this. The narrator in the one-acts and in *Our Town* is central to Friel's dramaturgy. The device is first found in *Lovers* in 1967 and subsequently — as the sociologist Dodds — in *The Freedom of the City* (1973). Thereafter the narrator evolves into the director Sir in *Living Quarters* (1977), into Michael, narrator *and* quasi-playwright in *Dancing at Lughnasa* (1990), and eventually into the form of the monologue play with *Faith Healer*. But the device is also boldly put to work in *The Loves of Cass McGuire* (1966), where Cass directly addresses the audience while remaining within the confines of naturalism.

Wilder's influence is also upon Friel's use of time and space, seen in the fluent way in which story-telling on stage can be telescoped and ironically inflected. Perhaps the *Freedom of the City* is in that regard indebted more to Wilder than to Brecht. More study needs to be given to this question. It is best inspected via Guthrie. He was an enthusiast. By the early 1960s Guthrie felt that *Our Town* had established itself worldwide 'as one of the hottest modern candidates for classical status.' He put the achievement in a nutshell: 'Wilder substitutes symbolism for naturalism, ritual for illusion, and discards elaborate scenery for a bare stage.'[38] Wilder was a playwright after his own heart. Guthrie directed a very successful production of *The Matchmaker* (forerunner of *Hello, Dolly!*) at the Edinburgh Theatre Festival in 1954, and once again it was the play's theatricalism Guthrie emphasised. This, too, was the theme of Wilder's own comments on his plays: 'Molière said that for the theatre all he needed was a platform and a passion or two. The climax of [*Our Town*] needs only five square feet of boarding and the passion to know what life means to us.'[39] It is hard not to think here of the simplicity of *mise en scène* called for in *Molly Sweeney* (1994), which Friel himself directed in its premiere: there were no props, just three chairs on the bare Gate stage, with a backdrop of cornflowers.

In the congruence of like minds Friel educated himself in the best modern theatrical production values by looking for models to Guthrie and Wilder at the same time. He met Wilder several times and liked him. And yet we have to accept that Friel was always his own man. As playwright he did not entirely share Wilder's sunny disposition, his insistence that even in the midst of death we are in life, even if only by the skin of our teeth. Friel's ironic take on life is darker, more pessimistic, and truer to the Irish — not to say Celtic — sensibility. And so, in spite of Guthrie's hearty endorsement Friel was by no means a slavish imitator. In some ways he was more conservative (there is no equivalent to *The Skin of Our Teeth* in Friel's work), in others more radically political. He could never be classified, as J.L. Styan classifies Wilder, among the expressionists. When all is said, Friel is closer to Chekhov in temperament and style. After all, his version of *Three Sisters* is the only one of Friel's texts to be re-published in a revised edition (Gallery Press, 2008). Thus, in the main, naturalism is Friel's metier whereas Wilder 'abandoned traditional staging and with the help of suggested myth and colloquial speech relied upon imagination.'[40] But Friel is Protean. His inspiration derives from multiple influences quietly internalised and transformed. Guthrie helped enormously to channel these early influences, which included the work of Wilder, and thus to enable his protégé to develop his genius for the stage.

## NOTES

[1] Tyrone Guthrie, *In Various Directions* (London: Michael Joseph, 1965), p. 173.
[2] Thornton Wilder, Preface to *Our Town, The Skin of Our Teeth, and The Matchmaker* (Harmondsworth: Penguin, 1962), pp. 12-14.
[3] D.E.S. Maxwell, *Brian Friel* (Lewisburg: Bucknell UP, 1973), p. 50.
[4] Brian Friel to Ria Mooney, 24 July 1962, Ria Mooney Papers, NLI accession no. 6548, Miscellaneous Letters to Ria Mooney, Box 2.
[5] Brian Friel, 'Self-Portrait (1972)', in *Essays, Diaries, Interviews: 1964-1999*, ed. Christopher Murray (London: Faber, 1999), p. 42.
[6] Brian Friel, 'Self-Portrait,' *Essays, Diaries, Interviews*, p. 144.
[7] Correspondence from Friel's agent Curtis Brown, 11 September 1963, Friel Papers, National Library of Ireland, MS 37, 048/1.
[8] Brian Friel Papers, National Library of Ireland, MS 37,048/1. Friel typed up a slightly edited version of Guthrie's letter, marked it 'Private' and annotated it with this comment and one other (regarding an epilogue).
[9] Tyrone Guthrie to Brian Friel, 11 October 1964, Friel Papers, NLI, MS 37, 048/1. *Philadelphia*, directed by Hilton Edwards, opened at the Gaiety Theatre as part of the Dublin Theatre Festival on 28 September 1964.
[10] In 'Self-Portrait' (1972), Friel says he gratefully accepted the term 'observer' conferred upon him by an actor in rehearsal after a doorman sought to expel Friel (see *Essays,*

*Diaries, Interviews*: 43). Much later, in a letter to Joe Dowling and the company of *Philadelphia, Here I Come!* at the Guthrie Theatre, dated 14 June 1996, Friel wrote that 'The play would never have been written had I not been an apprentice there under the great Tyrone Guthrie.' The letter was included in the 'Guthrie Program' for August 1996-97. I am grateful to the artistic director, Joe Dowling, for a copy of this theatre programme.

[11] Alfred Rossi, *Minneapolis Rehearsals: Tyrone Guthrie Directs Hamlet* (Berkeley: U. of California Press, 1970), pp. 3-70.

[12] In conversation with Brian Friel, 9 December 2008. He said 'all' rehearsals and perhaps that includes *Salesman* also.

[13] Richard Allen Cave, 'Friel's Dramaturgy: The Visual Dimension,' in *The Cambridge Companion to Brian Friel*, ed. Anthony Roche (Cambridge: CUP, 2006), p. 132.

[14] Joe Dowling, 'Staging Friel,' in *The Achievement of Brian Friel* (Gerrards Cross: Colin Smythe, 1993), p. 187.

[15] Brian Friel, *Selected Plays* (London: Faber, 1984), p. 426. Hereafter referred to in the text as *SP*.

[16] Richard Allen Cave, *Cambridge Companion*, 132, italics his.

[17] Brian Friel, 'Self-Portrait,' *Essays, Diaries, Interviews*, p. 42.

[18] Tyrone Guthrie, *A Life in the Theatre* (London: Hamish Hamilton, 1960), p. 301.

[19] Tyrone Guthrie, *In Various Directions*, p. 39.

[20] Brian Friel, responding to a speech of congratulation at Queen's University, Belfast (of which Tyrone Guthrie was once Chancellor) on the occasion of the dedication of the Brian Friel Theatre and Research Centre, 20 February 2009. Mike Wilcock, *Hamlet / The Shakespearean Director* (Dublin: Carysfort Press, 2002): 141-56, explores this relationship in Oedipal terms.

[21] Cited by Ulf Dantanus, *Brian Friel: The Growth of an Irish Dramatist* (Gothenburg: Acta Universitatis Gothoburgensis, 1985), p. 118.

[22] Denis Donoghue, 'A Reading of *Four Quartets*,' *The Ordinary Universe: Soundings in Modern Literature* (London: Faber and Faber, 1968), p. 260.

[23] Brian Friel, 'Seven Notes for a Festival Programme (1999),' *Essays, Diaries, Interviews*, p. 177.

[24] Friel, *Selected Plays*, 84, italics added. The subsequent quotation is from p. 88.

[25] Seamus Kelly, '*Volunteers* by Brian Friel at the Abbey,' *Irish Times*, 6 March 1975, p. 11.

[26] Seamus Heaney, 'Digging Deeper,' *Times Literary Supplement*, 23 March 1975: 306. Reprinted in *Preoccupations: Selected Prose 1968-1978* (London: Faber, 1980), pp. 214-16 (p. 214).

[27] Walter Benjamin, *Illuminations*, ed. Hannah Arendt, trans. Harry Zohn (London: Fontana, 1992), p. 248.

[28] Tyrone Guthrie, *A Life in the Theatre*, p. 130.

[29] Brian Friel, *Essays, Diaries, Interviews*, p. 111.

[30] Nicholas Grene, 'Five Ways of Looking at *Faith Healer*,' in *The Cambridge Companion to Brian Friel* p. 61.

[31] W. H. Auden, '*Musée des Beaux Arts*,' in *W.H. Auden: A Selection by the Author* (Harmondsworth: Penguin in association with Faber, 1958), p. 61.

[32] W. B.Yeats, *Essays and Introductions* (London and New York: Macmillan, 1961), p. 523.

[33] Brian Friel, *Essays, Diaries, Interviews*, p. 84.

[34] Tyrone Guthrie, 'On Three Productions,' *The Year's Work in the Theatre 1948-49* (London: Longmans Green for the British Council, 1949), pp. 31-2.

[35] Brian Friel, 'In Interview with Desmond Rushe (1970),' *Essays, Diaries, Interviews*, p.

31.

[36] J.L. Styan, *Modern Drama in Theory and Practice*, vol. 3, *Expressionism and Epic Theatre* (Cambridge; CUP, 1981), p. 115.

[37] Nicholas Grene, 'Friel and Transparency,' *Irish University Review*, 29.1 (1999), p. 139. See also Tony Corbett, *Brian Friel: Decoding the Language of the Tribe* (Dublin: Liffey Press, 2008), pp. 64, 84.

[38] Tyrone Guthrie, *In Various Directions*, pp. 111-12.

[39] Thornton Wilder, 'Preface,' p. 12.

[40] Walter J. Meserve, 'The dramatist and their plays,' in *The Revels History of Drama in English*, vol. VIII *American Drama*, ed. Travis Bogard, Richard Moody & Walter J. Meserve (London: Methuen, 1977), p. 271.

CHRISTOPHER MURRAY *is Professor Emeritus in the School of English, Drama and Film at University College Dublin. He is former editor of* Irish University Review *and former chair of the International Association for the Study of Irish Literatures (IASIL). Among his publications are* Twentieth Century Irish Drama: Mirror up to Nation *(Manchester: Manchester University Press, 1997; New York: Syracuse University Press, 2000) and* Sean O'Casey: Writer at Work *(Dublin: Gill & Macmillan, 2004).*

Irish Theatre International, Vol. 2, No. 1, pp. 28-37

# Changing the Direction of Theatre: Brian Friel's *Crystal and Fox* and John Osborne's *The Entertainer*

ANTHONY ROCHE

*Although the connection between Brian Friel and that of Russian playwrights Chekhov and Turgenev has been well flagged, not least by the playwright himself, what has rarely been noted is his creative engagement with British theatre of the mid-twentieth century. In the wake of the Belfast agreement, critics are beginning to speak more openly of this Irish playwright's crucial and intimate dialogue with contemporary British playwrights like John Osborne and Arnold Wesker and to recognize how Friel's plays never refrained from that necessary dialogue across the past half century. This article proposes an intertextual comparison of Friel's 1968 play,* Crystal and Fox, *and John Osborne's 1957* The Entertainer. *Friel views Osborne as a playwright of hope rather than anger and as someone who 'changed the direction of theatre' by striving to direct the medium 'away from Shaftesbury Avenue'. Accordingly, it is not Osborne's breakthrough play,* Look Back in Anger, *Friel most values but* The Entertainer *of the following year. Both make experimental use of traditional forms of theatre, Osborne of the English music-halls, Friel of the Irish fit-ups, the travelling theatres that toured rural areas offering a mix of melodrama, music and the circus. The central characters in each, Archie Rice and Fox Melarkey, are considered in detail as professional entertainers hiding existential ennui and despair behind the performer's mask. The casting of established classical actors Laurence Olivier and Cyril Cusack in those roles is examined. The article concludes by considering the politics of each play: where Osborne's play meditates on the break-up of the British Empire, Friel's is prescient on what is about to happen in the North.*

In the late 1950s, when Brian Friel began to write and have plays produced, there was very little in the contemporary local context to stimulate an apprentice playwright. Irish drama featured single successes like Brendan Behan's *The Quare Fellow* in 1954 and Sam Thompson's *Over the Bridge* in 1960 but nothing sustained.[1] Samuel Beckett was operating in a different language and culture, at too great a remove to have an immediate influence.[2] Closer to home John Osborne had inaugurated what, for better or worse, soon became known as the 'Angry Young Man' revolution. This movement helped to transform post-war British theatre, replacing the well-made plays of Terence Rattigan with something much more dishevelled and antagonistic to the established order. What has been all too rarely commented on is Friel's creative engagement with British theatre of the mid twentieth century, even though he has commented positively on many of the key names associated with that movement: 'I admire [...] a lot of English dramatists, [John] Osborne, [John]Arden and [Arnold] Wesker.'[3] The time is ripe for an act of historic recovery of a necessary and missing context for Friel's theatre and I think it no accident that critical attention is now being directed in that quarter. At the 2006 IASIL Conference in Sydney on the theme of intertextuality, Emilie Pine delivered a persuasive comparison of Friel's 1990 *Dancing at Lughnasa* and Arnold Wesker's 1958 *Chicken Soup with Barley*; and at the Magill Summer

School celebrating Friel in July 2008, Christopher Murray introduced a staged reading of 1961's *The Enemy Within* by referring to Robert Bolt's 1960 *A Man For All Seasons*. In this article, I wish to examine the intertextual connections between Friel's 1968 play, *Crystal and Fox*, and John Osborne's *The Entertainer* of 1957. What these comparisons suggest is that Brian Friel's dialogue with the contemporary British theatre may be the most sustained and searching of all. But it has only been possible, I think, in the wake of the Belfast Agreement to speak more openly of an Irish playwright in crucial and intimate dialogue with English dramatists and developments in English theatre and to recognize how Friel's plays never refrained from that necessary dialogue at any stage of the past half century.

It is not anger that Friel values in John Osborne but hope, as one of 'the optimistic people who happen to use black canvases'.[4] Osborne's achievement for Friel was that 'he changed the direction of theatre' by striving to direct the medium 'away from Shaftesbury Avenue'.[5] Accordingly, it is not *Look Back in Anger* the Irish playwright values most but *The Entertainer* of the following year. Osborne's play centres on the figure of Archie Rice, a fifty-year-old music hall entertainer who (like the medium in which he appears) is on his last legs. When he bemoans the condition of the audiences he has to confront and their lack of appreciation for what is on offer, his father Billy remembers that when he was a young performer, London audiences were the 'best audience in the world'.[6] Archie Rice is too young ever to have had that experience and turns instead for his rare occasion of a rapport between audience and performer to Ireland and the fit-ups. Archie's speech is one of the play's most memorable and amusing set-pieces, both referring to and exemplifying the theatre of which it speaks:

> I was in a little village in Donegal once. On the Irish fit-ups. (*To Billy*.) You remember. The morning we arrived there a man came up to me and said: "Oh, we're great students of the drama here. Great students of the drama. Our dramatic critics can lick anyone – anyone!" Turned out he was the local blacksmith. He said: "If you get past an audience here, you'll get past any audience in the world." It was true too. Think I got a black eye. (75)

Archie's speech is reminiscent of the more extensive sojourn of an English actor in the Irish fit-ups in the same decade. In the early 1950s, the playwright Harold Pinter was plying his earlier trade as an actor, touring Ireland as a member of Anew McMaster's troupe. Pinter's memoir *Mac* has a memorable account of a late-night drunken audience being brought to rapt and silent attention by Mc-Master's performance as Othello. The actor-manager remarks: 'But you see one thing the Irish peasantry really appreciate is style, grace and wit.'[7] In 1968, Brian Friel wrote a play, *Crystal and Fox*, about the fit-up companies that travelled around Ireland for decades, offering a mix of music, melodrama and circus acts. The Fox Melarkey Show presents, not the Shakespearean classics that McMaster offered fifteen years earlier, but the more down-market fare of popular melodramas modelled on contemporary movies. John Osborne and Harold Pinter both had their apprenticeship in the theatre as actors in the English touring repertory system and both seem to view the Irish fit-ups in rather a sentimental and nos-talgic light; for Pinter, his two years with McMaster in Ireland was 'a golden age for me and for others'.[8] Fox Melarkey, faced with the day-to-day experience as actor-manager of his troupe, takes a more cynical view of his audience, remark-ing at one point: 'Belt it out. And plenty of tears. All the hoors want is a happy end-ing.'[9] But as fellow Donegal playwright Frank McGuinness points out in relation to *Crystal and Fox*, 'it is with a deeply knowing comic irony that Friel, the most experimental dramatist of his generation, turned to this world as metaphor of his art.'[10] The same can be said of Osborne with *The Entertainer*. He is providing a conscious critique of the current state of British theatre through a self-conscious and ironic deployment of an earlier theatrical form, that of the music-hall. In his autobiography *A Better Class of Person* (1981), Osborne writes he was attracted to the form because it primarily appealed to 'emotions like jealousy, crude patri-otism, lost love, poverty, death,' but presented in 'short scenes of melodramatic information, sentiment and broad humour'.[11]

If *Look Back in Anger* was hailed as a triumph of social and dramatic re-alism, *The Entertainer* is anti-naturalistic and self-conscious in acknowledging its own theatricality. Archie Rice alternates between his role as a stand-up comedian addressing an audience and a beleaguered and philandering son, husband and father. Likewise, the play's setting alternates between the theatre where Archie is performing in the spotlight against a backcloth and the rented accommodation in the seaside resort where he lives with his wife Phoebe, father Billy and son Frank. There had been a strong measure of self-conscious theatricality in Brian Friel's de-cision to have the role of his young protagonist in 1964's *Philadelphia, Here I Come!* played not by one but by two actors, one presenting the public figure that the rest of the characters see, the other the private voice of his unconscious yearn-ings, doubts and desires. Gar Public is essentially no different from how the young son about to emigrate to the US in a more naturalistic drama would be repre-sented; with the silence pervading between son and father offset by exchanges with the affectionate housekeeper and visitors to the house. But the figure of Pri-vate Gar opens up another realm of dramatic possibility in his interchanges with his alter ego, one in which he can not only act out his Walter Mitty fantasies but address the conflicted emotions aroused by his decision to leave home. In Friel's next play, *The Loves of Cass McGuire* (1966), the title character at one point ad-dresses the audience directly and questions the title which her playwright has as-signed her; it is a moment worthy of Pirandello. But in *Crystal and Fox* the setting is itself inherently theatrical, pitched from the start in the liminal zone connect-ing the onstage and offstage areas between which the performers move and in which they live. Fox combines a number of theatrical functions, both directing and producing his actors in the plays; and when they lose the main actors in the troupe he also takes on the leading male role in the melodrama. Fox's primary on-stage role is as a master of ceremonies who controls and directs the audiences in their responses. In this, he most closely resembles Archie Rice. The role of pro-fessional entertainer played by Fox and Archie requires that they keep up a happy mood, smile their smiles and tell their jokes, many of them innuendo-laden and having 'the wife' or 'the mother-in-law' as their butt. Both are involved in a stream of cross-talk with unruly members of the audience:

> VOICE: Is it faked?
> FOX: 'Course it's faked! (*Laughter*)  (13)

In neither play do the boundaries between what happens on stage and what happens off between the characters remain water-tight; rather, they increasingly seep into each other. The bitter jokes Archie tells in a professional capacity about 'the wife' – 'My wife - my wife. Old Charlie knows her, don't you, Charlie?' (24) - increasingly reflect on his estranged relations with his own wife, Phoebe. She has given up accompanying him on the road and now works in Woolworth's while making frequent isolated trips to the local 'flea-pit' cinema. The fact that Archie has sexual liaisons with women younger than his daughter is an open secret between them – and in their personal lives, the gender of the sexual philanderer is the reverse of the onstage comic stereotype. In the domestic scenes, Phoebe drinks and talks a great deal about the life she might have had, while Archie looks on dispassionately. On stage, the punch line for a comic gag increasingly fails to compensate for the increasingly bitter accounts he delivers about 'my wife – not only is she stupid, not only is she stupid, but she's cold as well. Oh, yes, cold. She may look sweet, but she's a very cold woman, my wife. Very cold. Cold and stupid. She's what they call a moron glacee' (59).

*Crystal and Fox* contains a play-within-the-play, *The Doctor's Story*, closely modelled on the contemporary film, *The Nun's Story*. In both, the beautiful young nun finally succumbs to the blandishments of the handsome doctor and trades in her wimple so they can marry. At the start of Friel's play, 'Dr Giroux' is *'backstage'* helping 'Sister Petite Sancta' *'out of a nun's habit and into a gaudy floral dress'* (11). The couple go back on stage for an elaborate scene of leave-taking between the nun and her Mother Superior, played by Fox's wife Crystal, the company's star performer. The two plays start to intertwine as it becomes apparent from the backstage bickering that Tanya and her husband El Cid are simultaneously leaving the Fox Melarkey troupe to work for his rival, Dick Prospect. The comments made by Mother Superior about the 'years of dedication to our little mission hospital here in Lakula in Eastern Zambia' (15) also apply to the travelling theatre performers with an appositeness that the considerable irony cannot quite extinguish. Fox makes the parallel himself late in the play when, hitching a ride, he thanks the car that stops by saying: 'May God reward you for your years of dedication to our little missionary hospital here in Lakula in Eastern Tipperary' (57). Nor is he above quoting mock-Scripture to his players: 'Contentment lies in total obedience – St. Paul's epistle to the South Africans.' (24) In the months Brian Friel spent watching the process of theatre up close at the Guthrie Theatre in Minneapolis in 1963, the apprentice playwright wrote of what he took from the experience in the following terms: 'I learned a great deal about the iron discipline of theatre, and I discovered a dedication and a nobility and a selflessness that one associates with a theoretical priesthood.'[12] However travestied and ironised that metaphor is by the run-down fit-up company we behold, something of the dedication and visionary possibility Friel glimpsed in the theatrical life still

persists in their endeavours. That combination of transcendence and squalor will
be explored more fully in *Faith Healer* (1980), another play about a down-at-heel
theatrical trio struggling to rise above their tawdry circumstances. In the even
more reduced version of *The Doctor's Story* which opens Act Two of *Crystal and
Fox*, the mismatch of performer and part is grotesquely apparent. Fox now plays
the Mother Superior and Crystal Sister Petita Sancta. The line he directs at the de-
parting nun – 'Oh, my child, you look so young and so beautiful' (40) – is echoed
by Fox's remembering his first encounter with his then-beautiful young wife and
by his wish 'to die and wake up in heaven with Crystal' (36). But in the play's present, Crystal is at least twenty years older and more bruised by experience.  When
she comes offstage, the automatic compliments with which her husband greets
her – 'Beautiful, my love. (*He kisses her on the forehead*) Very moving. Gets me
here (*heart*)... every time' (11) – reflect as much on the present state of their mar-
riage as it does on their professional relationship.

Archie Rice and Fox Melarkey are both fifty years of age, and are experi-
encing a professional and personal crisis. The theatrical forms in which they have
traded for their entire careers are going under, not so much in competition with
the movies, where the live element of the stage will always provide a strong
counter-attraction, but in the face of the home entertainment that television can
provide. Here the ten years between the two plays is telling: in the UK by 1957, the
BBC was well established and the arrival of the commercial channel, ITV, in that
same year was about to increase the pressure; in Ireland, RTE only began in 1962
but by 1968 was a major cultural force in the lives of people in the Republic, often
in conjunction with UTV and BBC. Fox's response is to treat drama as an adjunct
to TV news by taking his players to an area where a disaster has been reported –
'a train crash or an explosion in a school' (26) - and trading in the sentiment
aroused by putting on a tragedy. The increased sensationalism which Archie's
music-hall drama has resorted to is the on-stage presence of nude women, for
which his monologues are now little more than a distraction and a delay.

But the result is the same in each case: dwindling audiences. As Archie
replies to his wife's solicitous enquiry when he finally gets home:

> No it wasn't all right at the theatre. Monday night there were sixty sad
> little drabs in, and tonight there were about two hundred sad little drabs.
> If we can open on Monday night at west Hartlepoole, it will be by very re-
> luctant agreement of about thirty angry people... (36)

In the face of Archie's growing despair at falling attendances Phoebe protests that
she doesn't want to end her life being put in a box in west Hartlepoole, or wher-
ever her husband happens to be playing that night. Fox appears to endorse Crystal's characteristic optimism, whenever their nightly attendance shows any slight
increase, that the good times will soon return. But his disillusionment breaks out
in the backstage jibes he directs at their audiences, or lack of them: 'Bloody cow-
boys!' (13) Rather than resist the inevitable tide of attrition, it becomes clear that
Fox is accelerating the process by deliberately and persistently driving away the
remaining members of the troupe. The husband and wife team are propelled even

further into the arms of a rival company when Fox denies them the top curtain-call they have agreed. The man-and-dog team of the sixty-year-old Pedro and Gringo is brutally terminated when the dog is fed a lethal dose of arsenic. When Pedro refuses point-blank to take over the role of the young doctor, Fox insists that Crystal's octogenarian father play the role, making grotesquely explicit the gerontocracy of the fit-up and its players by the late 1960s. Something similar happens in *The Entertainer*. Late in Osborne's play, it emerges that Archie, desperate to draw in more punters, is pressing his father Billy Rice – the only one to have some reputation as a performer – back into theatrical service. His daughter Jean warns prophetically that 'you're going to kill that old man just to save that no-good, washed-up, tatty show of yours' (82); and in his next solo appearance Archie does indeed confirm to his audience that 'Billy Rice will not appear tonight. Billy Rice will not appear again' (83). The cause-and-effect is less clearly established in *Crystal and Fox*. After Fox's insistence that Papa will play the part, the next we hear of the character is that he is in hospital, where he dies shortly afterwards. More of a back story is supplied in the 1977 RTE TV dramatization of the play, where a couple of lines are added to confirm that it was the strain of the old man having to go on stage in a theatrical role that caused his physical breakdown and landed him in the hospital.[13]

The casting of the central roles of Archie and Fox was crucial to the *raison d'être* of each play. The 1957 premiere of *The Entertainer* at the Royal Court was notable for the fact that Laurence Olivier, the most famous English actor of his generation, played the role. This was not classical or Shakespearean theatre; this was the work of the younger, more experimental playwrights and Olivier was risking a great deal in making the change. As Michael Billington puts it: 'Olivier's commitment to Osborne's play was a decisive moment in post-war British theatre',[14] signalling a momentous shift away from the formulaic fare of the West End towards the radical style and content associated with the Royal Court Theatre in Sloane Square. Billington's words on Osborne's importance echo those of Friel's quoted earlier. There is a decisive whiff of Archie Rice in a later Friel character, Teddy the cockney manager of faith healer Frank Hardy, and I think the connection is confirmed by Teddy's references to Laurence Olivier as one of 'the great artists' – 'there's only one Sir Laurence - right?'[15] The role of Fox in the original Gate Theatre production was taken by Cyril Cusack, probably Ireland's most famous actor at the time in both theatre and film. But Cusack was more associated with such classic Abbey Theatre playwrights as Synge and O'Casey rather than with any of the younger writers in the contemporary field. When Friel writes the following elaborate stage direction for the actor playing Fox – his '*eyes go flat and he hides behind a mask of bland simplicity and vagueness*' (19) – it is hard not to credit that the role was written with Cusack specifically in mind. Both characters, Archie Rice and Fox Melarkey, are professional performers with an extensive repertoire of theatrical moves, entertainers who can turn on the charm as required. They have been playing the role for so long that they have become emotionally disconnected, faking what they can no longer feel. It is a stretch for these established actors playing Archie and Fox when they are asked to go beyond and behind their traditional charm to convey a world-weariness, an existential ennui, as their world closes in around them. This unmasking is directly articulated by Archie Rice in the climactic moment when he asks his daughter to look behind the professional façade and deep into his eyes: 'you'll get yourself a technique. You can smile, darn you, smile, and look the friendliest jolliest thing in the world, but [...] look at my eyes. I'm dead behind those eyes.' (72) The deadness behind the eyes is apparent in the leering, iconic photo of Olivier on the cover of the Faber edition of *The Entertainer*.

When *Crystal and Fox* was first produced in Dublin, in November 1968, Gus Smith's review in *The Irish Press* pointed out that Fox 'is reminiscent of Archie Rice in John Osborne's *The Entertainer*' and further argued that Cyril Cusack, 'as the cunning fox, does for this Friel work what Laurence Olivier did for *The Entertainer* – kept the drama alive.'[16] In his otherwise extremely positive review of play and production, Alec Reid thought Cusack's performance caught 'every nuance of the part' so far as portraying 'the little, crooked, self-centred chancer' but that the tragic dimension eluded him.[17] Perhaps professionally piqued by this review, Cusack returned to the role on television seven years later and delivered one of the most complex and moving portrayals of his career. The 'mask of bland simplicity and vagueness' was turned towards the other characters; but in isolated and isolating close-ups Cusack used his experience of film acting to deploy understatement and minimal facial and bodily gestures to suggest a tragic subtext. This interior mining of the part fed directly into those rare occasions when Fox lets slip the mask of the professional entertainer and confesses to his wife or son:

> Once, maybe twice in your life, the fog lifts, and you get a glimpse, an intuition; and suddenly you know that this can't be all there is to it – there has to be something better than this. (47)

The two plays are catalysed by the entrance of a missing family member and it is that entrance which brings an explicitly political context to the drama – or rather brings out its politics. In *The Entertainer*, Archie's daughter Jean arrives unexpectedly, having come to a point of crisis in her relationship with her fiancé. Their increasingly discordant views have surfaced over Jean's decision to attend a rally in Trafalgar Square opposing British involvement in Suez. Her grandfather Billy is appalled – 'that's what comes of giving them [women] the vote' (28) – and the news generates heated argument when the other family members hear about it. What stokes the debate is the fact that the brother we see in the company of his father is a conscientious objector while the other brother, Mick, who remains unseen throughout, is a member of the British troops in Egypt advancing into the Canal Zone. During the course of the play, the Rice family learns that Mick is first taken prisoner and then released; expected home as a hero, he returns in a coffin and the play concludes with his funeral. These scenes provide ironic contrast to the pro-Empire songs of the music hall which Archie sings on stage to work up some enthusiasm in the audience: 'Those bits of red still on the map/ We won't give up without a scrap.' (33) The only authentic performer Archie has ever seen is an old American black woman who sang the blues; and the blues lament he sings for his dead son is in a very different key from his usual musical fare. But even this dirge is underscored by the love of England which suffused everything Osborne wrote: 'But ain't no use agrievin'/'Cos it's Britain we believe in. (74).

In *Crystal and Fox*, we have the first of the returned prodigal sons that are to become such a feature of Friel's plays. Gabriel appears unexpectedly halfway through the First Act but the circumstances which have caused him to leave England and return to Ireland are so serious that Fox insists they keep the full details from Crystal. Like his father with his rickety wheel of fortune, Gabriel is a gambler and in his drifter's life abroad has accumulated a heavy quantity of debts. Interrupted in the middle of an act of petty larceny, he has struck out repeatedly at the shop owner and fears he has killed her. This fear is confirmed when two British detectives arrive in Act Two looking to extradite him. Even before the entrance of Gabriel, the travelling theatre has been approached by a local Garda who castigates them as itinerants and warns them to move on. Fox's instincts are to appease the policeman; Crystal's to oppose him. But these instincts are sharpened when the Garda and British detectives arrive to apprehend their son. Gabriel seeks to flee and, when apprehended, is dealt a blow *'in the lower stomach'* and warned: 'that's only the beginning, Paddy' (49). The prisoner is brought to Manchester for questioning in relation to the manslaughter and his mother Crystal declares she is determined to follow.

If Osborne's *Entertainer* meditates on the break-up of the British Empire, Friel's *Crystal and Fox* is prescient on what is about to happen in the North. In the altered political conditions of 1974 the TV dramatization of the play cut the dialogue of the two British detectives and restricted their activities to the arrest operation. The collusion between the Donegal garda and the police from the British mainland remains in place, however, and suggests the 'Heavy Gang' procedures that were to emerge in the following decade. But Gabriel is given no political justification for his manslaughter in either version; there is no suggestion that he is a member of the IRA or of any dissident political organization. While in prison in England, he has been assessed and diagnosed by a psychiatrist: 'And do you know what he said, Fox? He said I was autistic – "unable to responds emotionally to people". Funny word – autistic – isn't it?' (37) The reminiscences between the other players in the troupe establish the closeness that existed between father and son before a row blew up between Gabriel and his father. The emotional change in Fox, from natural ebullience and optimism to an ever more corrosive cynicism, is aligned with the moment of his son's departure and disappearance. It soon becomes clear that Gabriel's return, either way, is only temporary. And the process of attrition is complete when Fox casts off Crystal, by telling her the one thing even her loyalty will not forgive: that he was the one who handed their son over to the police, even though this is not true.

Fox is left alone at the end, at that most liminal of all settings: a crossroads, with a sign pointing in four directions, identified from Fox's perspective as 'Dublin – Galway – Cork – Derry' (56). According to his own estimate, 'he is at the hub of the country' in this lonely road in the wilds of Donegal. At the time of the play's first production, political events on the island were fast approaching crisis point. In Friel's own development, the success in the US which had attended both

*Philadelphia, Here I Come!* and *Lovers* posed the same dilemma he had diagnosed in John Osborne: a need to turn the direction of his theatre away from Broadway (rather than Shaftesbury Avenue) and to strike out in a chancier, riskier direction. The next decade would be a difficult and isolating one for the dramatist. The challenging and experimental plays he wrote in the late 1960s and throughout the 1970s opened to a very different reception from the acclaim which greeted those earlier plays and which would subsequently attend the premieres of *Translations* and *Dancing at Lughnasa*; but he could not have written those later plays had he not changed the direction of his theatre in plays like *Crystal and Fox*. As Frank McGuinness has put it, in writing these 'rabid, devious texts', Friel was not in the business of taming monsters here. Rather he unleashed them.[18]

NOTES

[1] By 1960, the Irish scene was being transformed by the emergence of a generation of outstanding contemporary playwrights: Tom Murphy, John B. Keane, Hugh Leonard in addition to Friel.
[2] The longer-term effects were considerable, as Beckett's plays circulated and were produced in English. See Anthony Roche, *Contemporary Irish Drama: Second Edition* (Basingstoke: Palgrave Macmillan, 2009), *passim.*
[3] Brian Friel, 'In Interview with Desmond Rushe' (1970), in Christopher Murray (editor) *Brian Friel: Essays, Diaries, Interviews: 1964-1999* (London and New York: Faber and Faber, 1999), p. 31.
[4] Brian Friel, 'In Interview with Des Hickey and Gus Smith' (1972), Murray, p. 48.
[5] Brian Friel, 'In Interview with Graham Morrison' (1965), Murray, p. 5.
[6] John Osborne, *The Entertainer* (London: Faber and Faber, 1957, 1995), p. 75. All future references to *The Entertainer* are to this edition and will be incorporated in the text.
[7] Harold Pinter, 'Mac', in *Various Voices: Prose, Poetry, Politics 1948-2005* (London: Faber and Faber, 2005), pp. 27-28.
[8] Pinter,'Mac', *Various Voices*, p. 33.
[9] Brian Friel, *Crystal and Fox* (Dublin: The Gallery Press, 1970, 1984), p. 13. All future references to *Crystal and Fox* are to this edition and will be incorporated in the text.
[10] Frank McGuinness, 'Surviving the 1960s: three plays by Brian Friel 1968-1971', in Anthony Roche (editor), *The Cambridge Companion to Brian Friel* (Cambridge: Cambridge University Press, 2006), p. 19.
[11] Cited in Christopher Innes, *Modern British Drama: The Twentieth Century* (Cambridge: Cambridge University Press, 2002), pp. 92-93.
[12] Brian Friel, 'Self-Portrait', Murray, p. 42.
[13] *Crystal and Fox* (Radio Telefis Eireann, 1977); director: Noel O Briain; screenplay: Brian Friel; starring Cyril Cusack, Maureen Toal, Cecil Sheridan.
[14] Michael Billington, *State of the Nation: British Theatre Since 1945* (London: Faber and Faber, 2007), p.108.
[15] Brian Friel, *Faith Healer: Plays: One* (London and Boston: Faber and Faber, 1996), p. 355.
[16] Gus Smith, review of *Crystal and Fox*, *The Irish Press*, November 13, 1968.
[17] Alec Reid, review of *Crystal and Fox*, *Social and Personal*, December 1968.
[18] Frank McGuinness, 'Surviving the 1960s', p. 28.

Anthony Roche *is Associate Professor in the School of English, Drama and Film at University College Dublin. From 1998 to 2002 he edited the* Irish University Review, *including Special Issues on Brian Friel (1999) and Thomas Kilroy (2002). Recent publications include the chapter on 'Contemporary Drama in English: 1940-2000' in Margaret Kelleher and Philip O'Leary (editors),* The Cambridge History of Irish Literature Volume II: 1890-2000 *(2006) and* The Cambridge Companion to Brian Friel *(2006). A revised, expanded and updated edition of his book,* Contemporary Irish Drama, *will appear from Palgrave Macmillan in 2009; he is currently writing a book entitled* Brian Friel: Theatre and Politics, *to be published by Palgrave Macmillan in 2010. He has also completed* Synge and the Making of a Modern Irish Drama, *which will appear from Carysfort Press in 2010.*

Irish Theatre International, Vol. 2, No. 1, pp. 38-47
©Irish Society for Theatre Research, 2009. Printed in the Republic of Ireland.

# Brian Friel and the Sovereignty of Language

Nicholas Grene

*In spite of Brian Friel's reverence for the superior expressiveness of music, in spite of his awareness of the deficiencies of the word, he creates a theatre dependent on the persuasive powers of language. He may not use the dialect high colour of a Synge or O'Casey; in his plays not every speech is 'as fully flavoured as a nut or apple'. Nonetheless, Friel belongs within that tradition of verbal drama in which Irish-English speech is valued for its comic fluency, its story-telling inventiveness and its lyrical grace. An audience, if they are to be held in Friel's theatre, must at key moments trust in language, go with its flow. It is language at such points, not music, not dance, that is sovereign.*

'The people who huckster in words merely report on feeling. We *speak* feeling'.[1] So speaks Janacek the composer in *Performances*, asserting the supremacy of music as artistic medium; the verb 'huckster' enforces the musician's contempt for the mere litterateur who stands at a derivative remove from the direct expressiveness of his own art. The structure of Friel's play serves to endorse Janacek's view. The naive attempt by the researcher Anezka to establish Janacek's love relationship with Kamila Stosslova as the source for his Second String Quartet is counteracted not only by the composer's own rebuttal of her theories, but by the onstage playing of the quartet itself. The music silences the mere words of the play. This is not the only work in which Friel seems to affirm the superiority of music over his own language-based art of drama. As Harry White puts it in a persuasive article, 'his plays advance the case for music as a symbolic force which can usurp the function of language and which, on occasion, can determine the structural coherence of the drama itself'.[2] Music is a key element in several of his plays, most notably in *Aristocrats* where the crucially important Chopin piano pieces required in each act are specified.[3] In *Wonderful Tennessee*, George, who is dying of throat cancer and unable to speak, expresses with his accordion the feelings of the whole group of friends astray on the Donegal pier. There is in Friel some of that envy of the singer that is a crucial motive factor in Tom Murphy's drama.[4] Words are shoddy, imprecise, broken tools; language is a mere pretender to the realm in which music is sovereign.

If language in Friel is often thus poor stepsister to music as an artistic medium, it is also problematic as a means of communication. *Translations*, with its theatrical device of mutual incomprehension between the Irish speakers of Ballybeg and the Anglophone soldiers, creates a drama of miscomprehension. The well-intentioned English army officer Yolland is resigned to the fact that 'Even if I did speak Irish I'd always be an outsider here, wouldn't I? I may learn the password but the language of the tribe will always elude me, won't it? The private core will always be ... hermetic' (*Plays 1*, 416). The difficulty is not only that of communicating meaning accurately from one language to another. Friel follows his theoretical source for *Translations*, George Steiner's *After Babel*, in suggesting a fundamental opacity in language that makes ultimately impossible the task of 'interpret[ing] between privacies' (*Plays 1*, 446). In *The Communication Cord*, Friel puts linguistics at the centre of his absurd situation farce. Tim is a research student in discourse analysis working on 'response cries', those elements in language which have least information content, that communicate, if at all, at some non-linguistic level.[5] This deepens and theorizes the standard tropes of farce: pretences, mistaken identities and the systematic subversion of normal conversational exchanges. Friel's 'language plays', as they have been called, dramatize the inadequacies of language, its fragility and its inbuilt tendency to dysfunction.[6]

Yet, of course, Friel is an eloquent playwright who endows many of his characters with much of his own eloquence. In spite of his reverence for the superior expressiveness of music, in spite of his awareness of the deficiencies of the word, he creates a theatre dependent on the persuasive powers of language. His mission is never, like that of Beckett, to bring language into disrepute.[7] He may not use the dialect high colour of a Synge or O'Casey; in his plays not every speech is 'as fully flavoured as a nut or apple'.[8] Nonetheless, Friel belongs within that tradition of verbal drama in which Irish-English speech is valued for its comic fluency, its story-telling inventiveness and its lyrical grace. An audience, if they are to be held in Friel's theatre, must at key moments trust in language, go with its flow. It is language at such points, not music, not dance, that is sovereign.

The fluency and eloquence is most striking in Friel's breakthrough success, *Philadelphia Here I Come!*, because that is a play so centrally concerned with tongue-tied inarticulacy: Gar and his father are equally unable to voice their thoughts and emotions. On the surface, indeed, it could be seen as some sort of protest against the Syngean tradition glorifying the 'popular imagination that is fiery and magnificent, and tender'.[9] S.B.'s speech runs to nothing more fiery or magnificent that the daily repeated observation 'Another day over' (*Plays 1*, 48), or remarks about the decline in the number of rats in the shop storeroom. The claustrophobically lifeless community of Ballybeg, from the Canon and the Master to the self-consciously boisterous 'boys', expresses itself in the tiredest, the most inert and inane sort of public language. However, in inventing Private Gar as the shadow self of his Public counterpart, Friel opens up a whole other register of language to offset the drabness of the actual voiced speech of the village. In Private, the unspoken is spoken, subtext becomes a free-flowing, articulate overtext. A comic fantasia is made to play about the numbing ordinariness of the ordinary. The nightly ritual of S.B., hat always on head, coming from the shop to the tea-table, is accompanied by Private's spoof fashion-parade commentary: 'And this time Marie Celeste is wearing a cheeky little head-dress by Pamela of Park Avenue ...' (*Plays 1*, 47). When faced with the socially superior Senator Doogan, father of Gar's girl-friend Kate, Public Gar has not a word to say for himself. But Private can take satirical revenge on Doogan's effortless suppression of the romance: 'You know, of course, that he carries one of those wee black cards in the inside pocket of his jacket, privately printed for him: "I am a Catholic. In case of accident send for a bishop"' (*Plays 1*, 45). Wit, verbal facility, comic fluency, the very qualities that Public so signally lacks, are richly allowed to Private. The strategy is, of course, theatrically winning: the audience can observe the stultifying boredom of Ballybeg while revelling in the exuberant entertainment offered by its unobserved internal commentator.

In *Philadelphia,* Friel uses Private as both Walter Mitty-like comic fantasist and as critical truth-teller. Other characters, such as the irrepressibly irresponsible Frank in *Molly Sweeney,* are more consistently unreliable narrators; Frank's various 'schemes', for making cheese from Iranian goats, or importing African bees, all described with the same manic optimism, are clearly as doomed as his mission to cure his wife of blindness. With Frank and Private Gar, Friel makes capital out of the sheer unstoppable flow of language. There are, however, also in Friel, reliable narrators who tell nothing but the plain, objective truth. So, for example, in 'Winners', the first of the two one-act plays that make up the diptych *Lovers,* the Commentators, seated at the edge of the stage, read from a script that give the audience the facts of the story: 'Their reading is impersonal, completely without emotion: their function is to give information'.[10] Here the designed dramatic effect appears to be to show the inadequacy of such dispassionate narration to render the reality of the two young lovers we see on stage in all their complex lived vitality. In *Living Quarters,* the objective narrator is put to a very different use. 'Sir' bears the ledger in which the truths of what happened on the day of Frank Butler's suicide are inscribed. The Pirandello-like drama involves the constant attempts of the individual characters to re-write their own role in the script, to soften the focus on their parts in the action, to shift the burden of blame elsewhere. Each time Sir, gently but inescapably, pulls them back to the documented reality of the ledger. This is narrative as immutable tragic fate. The omniscience of Sir and the neutrality of his God-like narrative style make for a theatrical problem. Where Private Gar's verbal arabesques enlivened the otherwise banal social surfaces of Ballybeg, Sir's choric voice is humanly dead in its unflappable infallibility. Still, the device is a testimony to Friel's felt need for a trustworthy language in the theatre that stands above the dissimulations and distortions of his characters' voices.

In some of Friel's plays he has tried, as it were, to compensate his characters for the deficiencies in their lives and their language. In *The Loves of Cass McGuire,* the three central characters living in the old people's home, Trilbe, Ingram and Cass herself, are given 'rhapsodies' in which they sit in the winged chair and create 'counterfictions', romanticized versions of their past lives.[11] Supported by background music from Wagner, and the reading of the legend of the doomed lovers Tristan and Iseult, Trilbe and Ingram help one another to tell their 'stories'. Cass McGuire, returned emigrant from New York, drunken hell-raiser, outrageous embarrassment to her respectable family, is initially resistant to the fantasizing game of the other two. By the end though, she too is lured into the winged chair, and starts into her own counterfiction:

> I stood at the stern of the ship, and two white and green lines spread out and out and out before me. And the gentleman I worked for, Mr. Olsen, he was only a few years older than me, tall and straight and manly, with golden hair and kind soft patient eyes.[12]

In his 'Author's Note' Friel makes clear the deliberateness of his choice of the musical term 'rhapsody' and the intended effect: 'Each of the three characters who rhapsodize ... takes the shabby and unpromising threads of his or her past life and weaves it into a hymn of joy, a gay and rapturous and exaggerated celebration of a beauty that might have been'.[13] For all the florid inauthenticity of this rhapsodic rhetoric, Friel invites audience sympathy, even respect, for his characters' ecstatic self-imagining.

*The Freedom of the City* represents a very different case. The actual drama of the three unwitting civil rights marchers caught accidentally in the Derry Guildhall is played out against a montage of spectacular misrepresentations of their lives and deaths: the tribunal investigation into their killing that frames the play, the evidently partisan myth-making of the Balladeer, the politically influenced funeral addresses of the priest, the superficialities of the TV reporter. For good measure, Friel throws in an unrelated lecture by the sociologist Dodds on the 'subculture of poverty'; his academic generalizations are ironically illustrated by the characters of Lily, Michael and Skinner, whose last hours we are witnessing. The whole dramatic effect of the play depends on the counterpointing of these variously false and distorted discourses with the real lives of the three working-class Derry people as we see them played out live in front of us. Yet strikingly, at the very moment of death, Friel gives to each of the three of them a final formal utterance in which 'they speak calmly, without emotion, in neutral accents' (*Plays 1*, 149). In one sense, the characters react characteristically: the well-intentioned upright Michael believes to the end that their shooting must be a mistake; the instinctual Lily can sense immediately that she is about to die – 'Jesus, they're going to murder me'; the cynical Skinner remains cynical to the last, dying as he lived 'in defensive flippancy' (*Plays 1*, 150). However, in these speeches Friel accords to the characters a degree of understanding that they never attained in their lives, and a language not their own in which to voice it. Lily's speech is the most striking, as she experienced 'a second of panic, no more':

> Because it was succeeded, overtaken, overwhelmed by a tidal wave of regret, not for myself nor my family, but that life had somehow eluded me. And now it was finished; it had all seeped away; and I had never experienced it. And in the silence before my body disintegrated in a purple convulsion, I thought I glimpsed a tiny truth: that life had eluded me because never once in my forty-three years had an experience, an event, even a small unimportant happening been isolated, and assessed, and articulated. (*Plays 1*, 150)

This is Brian Friel's perception of the tragedy of Lily, not her own. And the organization of the speech – the controlled syntax and cadences of the sentences, the succession of triads from 'succeeded, overtaken, overwhelmed' to 'isolated, and assessed, and articulated' – is that of the skilled writer so unlike Lily's normal Derry demotic. As a matter of human dignity, Friel wants his character to be granted a moment of tragic realisation and to voice it he lends her his own verbal skills.

Everywhere in Friel's drama there are story-tellers, monologuists, narrators, reliable and spectacularly unreliable. Nowhere is the issue of the degree of reliability more central than in *Faith Healer*. Through Frank's first monologue, an audience new to the play would have no reason to distrust the speaker. The opening of the speech with the incantation of the names of 'all those dying Welsh villages', the vivid evocation of the out of the way places where he 'performed', is broken off by a convincingly ironic self-introduction: 'I beg your pardon – *The Fantastic Francis Hardy, Faith Healer, One Night Only. (A slight bow.)* The man on the tatty banner'. (*Plays 1*, 332). We are held all the more by his self-narration because of what appears to be his struggle to define his faith healing precisely and honestly:

> Faith healer – faith healing. A craft without an apprenticeship, a ministry without responsibility, a vocation without a ministry. How did I get involved? As a young man I chanced to flirt with it and it possessed me. No, no, no, no, no – that's rhetoric. No; let's say I did it ... because I could do it. That's accurate enough. (*Plays 1*, 333)

Frank's reaction against 'rhetoric' here authenticates what is in fact his own very artful storytelling. We have, for instance, no cause to doubt his casual characterization of 'Grace, my mistress. A Yorkshire woman. Controlled, correct, methodical, orderly' (*Plays 1*, 335).

The shock is all the greater, therefore, when Frank disappears from the stage, and his place is taken by Grace, Grace who insists that she was Frank's wife – it was merely a cruel pretence of his to say they were not married – and who is as Irish as he is. What is more, the woman we see is anything but controlled, correct and methodical: she is in breakdown, drinking, chain-smoking, 'barely concealing her distraught mental state' (*Plays 1*, 341). In fact, it is the very fragmented and disorderly nature of her speech, her pathetic and evidently hopeless efforts to reassure herself – 'I *am* getting stronger, I *am* becoming more controlled – I'm sure I am' (*Plays 1*, 341) – that lend credence to her monologue. By contrast with the mellifluous persuasiveness of Frank's assured performance, the broken sentences of Grace's tormented self-examination convince an audience by the very lack of control. As a result, we are disposed to believe her version of things: that she *was* married to Frank, not his mistress, that she *did* come from Ireland not Yorkshire, that she gave birth to a stillborn baby in Kinlochbervie, an event Frank never acknowledges happened. Frank, whose first monologue completely convinced the audience, is now seen to be an inveterate mythmaker, driven by 'some compulsion he had to adjust, to refashion, to re-create everything around him' (*Plays 1*, 345).

We then hear from Teddy, the business manager, third of the trio. Teddy is the showman, his style that of the unbuttoned showbiz reminiscence, and an audience, recognizing the genre, will make large allowances for its truth content. It seems improbable that the previous 'performers' he handled, 'Rob Roy, The Piping Dog', and 'Miss Mulatto and Her Pigeons', were quite the famous sensations he claims. His frequently repeated assertion that the manager must treat his clients 'on the basis of a relationship that is strictly business only' (*Plays 1*, 357) is obviously ironic in view of his deeply emotional involvement with both Frank and Grace. His speech, however, supplies a third perspective on the tragic events that culminated in Frank's murder and Grace's suicide, in incompatible conflict with both of the other two accounts at different points. Held as we are in the theatre by the speaking presence of the three monologuists in turn, by the end of Teddy's part we seem to be left only with a sense of the inevitable distortions of memory, the subjectivities of speech and perception, that make truth inherently undecidable.

But then there is Frank's second monologue with which the play ends. The effect here is different, and it is interesting to try to establish why it should be so. It is not that Frank is more inherently trustworthy at this point. He continues to persist in statements that, on the basis of the testimony of the other two characters, we must consider untrue. 'I would have liked to have had a child', he says; 'But she was barren' (*Plays 1*, 372). Both Grace and Teddy have remembered the stillbirth in Kinlochbervie (however differently in detail) so this has to be taken as a wilful denial on Frank's part. Frank's recollections in this monologue – of his last encounter with Grace's mother as a mental patient, of a humiliating incident with his own father at Ballinasloe horse fair – may be true or false, there is no way of knowing. But the mood of Frank himself is changed from the first monologue, as the stage direction indicates: he is 'slightly less aloof, not quite as detached' and 'there should be tenuous evidence of a slightly heightened pulse-rate, of something approximating to excitement in him' (*Plays 1*, 370). There is a change in the set also; the poster which was the play's most significant prop is gone, as are all the chairs but the one on which Frank cast his coat when starting his first speech. He is left completely on his own. The only part of the story that no-one has told in full before is the murder itself, and an audience in the theatre will realise that is what they are now going to hear from Frank.

We hear it and at least partially see it enacted. Frank remembers how he kept the newsclipping testifying to his miraculous cures in Llanbethian. 'And that night in that pub in Ballybeg I crumpled it up (*He does this now*) and threw it away' (*Plays 1*, 371). The action is again suited to the words as he describes pacing the floor of the pub waiting for the wedding guests to return with the hopelessly paralysed McGarvey. When he prepares to tell how he went out into the yard where McGarvey and his friends are waiting for him, where he is to be killed when he fails in his attempt at a cure, he 'puts on the hat and overcoat and buttons it slowly' (*Plays 1*, 374). Narration here moves towards acted drama while still remaining narration; Frank may put on his outdoor clothes but the description that follows, of the space outside the pub, the yard in which he finds the men who are to be his murderers, the instruments with which they will kill him, is told in words alone from the bare stage. Friel's reliance on language here was the more striking in a theatrical production that attempted something different. Joe Dowling, who directed the first brilliant Irish staging of *Faith Healer* in 1980 with Donal McCann in the lead, revived the play, again with McCann, in 1990. In the revival, the last stages of the final monologue were supported by back projected images of the yard, with Frank appearing actually to move off stage into the space he describes. For this audience member at least, it seemed like a failure of trust in the effect of the language and the actor that had worked to such magnificent effect in the earlier production.

The concluding passages of Frank's monologue are designed to be beyond doubt, beyond disbelief. This is the tragic protagonist meeting his fate with the authority and the conviction that is granted only to such a figure at such a terminal moment of the drama:

> As I walked I became possessed of a strange and trembling intimation: that the whole corporeal world – the cobbles, the trees, the sky, those four malign implements – somehow they had shed their physical reality and had become mere imaginings, and that in all existence there was only myself and the wedding guests. And that intimation in turn gave way to a stronger sense: that even we had ceased to be physical and existed only in spirit, only in the need we had for each other.
> *(He takes off his hat as if he were entering a church and holds it at his chest. He is both awed and elated. As he speaks the remaining lines he moves very slowly down stage.)*
> And as I moved across that yard towards them and offered myself to them, then for the first time I had a simple and genuine sense of homecoming. Then for the first time there was no atrophying terror; and the maddening questions were silent.
> At long last I was renouncing chance. (*Plays 1*, 375-6)

This has been prepared for all through the text as the play's resolving chord: the 'maddening questions' were those that had tormented Frank about the genuineness of his faith healing gift; he is 'renouncing chance' because, in his acceptance of failure and death, he is no longer at the mercy of the arbitrariness of his talent. This final experience is appropriately rendered through language alone because it is a transfiguration of the material into 'mere imaginings' which no theatrical embodiment could enact. The design of the speech is to leave an audience in the theatre unable to resist Frank's mood of awe and elation or the eloquence with which his secular martyrdom is so powerfully expressed.

If Friel, himself one of those who 'huckster in words', paid tribute to the superiority of music as a medium in *Performances*, he put dancing at the centre of what must still probably be his most famous play. The dancing of *Dancing at Lughnasa,* with its remembered 1930s setting stood for everything that orthodox Catholic Ireland had repressed, above all the vitality of women's bodies. With its first performance in 1990, Terence Brown has placed it as one of the signs of the new decade: 'Friel's play … seemed to serve notice that in Ireland's post-colonial experience … the energies of women could not be easily contained in conventional, patriarchal versions of the social order.'[14] Father Jack's ecstatic evocation of an East African religious festival, parallel to the ancient Irish pagan festival of Lughnasa, reinforces the point:

We light fires around the periphery of the circle; and paint our faces with coloured powders; and we sing local songs; and we drink palm wine. And then we dance – and dance – and dance – children, men, women, most of them lepers, many of them with misshapen limbs, with missing limbs – dancing, believe it or not, for days on end!  It is the most wonderful sight you have ever seen.[15]

The carnival of the pagan community, with its uninhibited celebration of the body, stands as antithetical opposite to the severe Christian cult of the Word. The wildly explosive dance of the Mundy sisters in Act I is the theatrical embodiment of this.

Of course, *Dancing at Lughnasa* is a memory play; the actions on stage are mediated through the narrative of the middle-aged Michael recollecting the experiences of his seven-year-old self: 'When I cast my mind back to that summer of 1936 different kinds of memory offer themselves to me'. (*Plays 2*, 7) It is he who gives us a foretaste of the women's dance in his opening monologue, though he is not actually present on stage when it is performed:[16] 'I remember the kitchen throbbing with the beat of Irish dance music beamed to us all the way from Dublin, and my mother and her sisters suddenly catching hands and dancing a spontaneous step-dance and laughing – screaming! – like excited schoolgirls'. (*Plays 2*, 8) This scene when it comes makes a huge theatrical impact, and I can remember at the first night of the play in the Abbey Theatre being surprised that Act II brought no comparable climax. According to a conventional expectation of the strategies of the theatre, a first act sensation should be topped by a second act counterpart. It is the expectation fulfilled in the fully visual medium of the cinema, where Pat O'Connor's 1998 film version of *Dancing at Lughnasa* ends with a reprise of the women's dance. In the play, by contrast, Friel concentrates the visual effect on a repeated tableau, the characters as we saw them frozen in Michael's idealizing memory at the beginning of the play, now in 'soiled and shabby' versions of themselves, with 'a crude, cruel, grinning face, primitively drawn, garishly painted' on each of the kites the boy Michael has made, here seen for the first time. (*Plays 2*, 106) The harshness of this spectacle, however, is offset by the 'very soft, golden light' by which it is viewed, and the extraordinary beauty of Michael's last monologue in which he speaks of his memories in which 'atmosphere is more real than incident and everything is simultaneously actual and illusory'.

When I remember it, I think of it as dancing.  Dancing with eyes half closed because to open them would break the spell.  Dancing as if language had surrendered to movement – as if this ritual, this wordless ceremony, was now the way to speak, to whisper private and sacred things, to be in touch with some otherness.  Dancing as if the very heart of life and all its hopes might be found in those assuaging notes and those hushed rhythms and in those silent and hypnotic movements.  Dancing as if language no longer existed because words were no longer necessary ... (*Plays 2*, 108)

It must be one of the most mesmerically lyrical conclusions to any modern play. Michael's vision in which 'everything is simultaneously actual and illusory' is some sort of equivalent to Frank's ghostly re-creation of his last moments in *Faith Healer*. But the paradoxes of the speech are obvious. 'Dancing as if language had surrendered to movement': it hasn't, quite the opposite – language is taking the place of movement. 'Dancing as if language no longer existed because words were no longer necessary': but they are necessary, precisely to express this languageless state. In Friel's theatrical universe, where direct action is relatively rare, where drama is typically rendered through the distorting lenses of storytelling and memory, it is only through language, fragile and unreliable as it may be, that the deepest levels of meaning can be figured.

NOTES

[1] Brian Friel, *Performances* (Oldcastle: Gallery, 2003), p. 31.
[2] Harry White, 'Brian Friel and the Condition of Music', *Irish University Review*, 29.1 (1999), 6-15, (p. 6).
[3] Brian Friel, *Plays 1* (London: Faber & Faber, 1996), p. 251. This is the text used for all further quotations from plays contained in it, with references given parenthetically in the text.
[4] See Tom Murphy in conversation with Michael Billington in Nicholas Grene (ed.), *Talking about Tom Murphy* (Dublin: Carysfort, 2002), p. 105.
[5] Brian Friel, *The Communication Cord* (London: Faber, 1983), p. 18.
[6] Richard Kearney groups *Translations* with *The Communication Cord* and *Faith Healer* as 'The Language Plays of Brian Friel' in *Transitions: Narratives in Modern Irish Culture* (Manchester: Manchester University Press, 1988), pp. 123-60.
[7] 'As we cannot eliminate language all at once, we should at least leave nothing undone that might contribute to its falling into disrepute', Samuel Beckett, *Disjecta* (London: John Calder, 1983), p. 172.
[8] J.M. Synge, *Plays*, ed. Ann Saddlemyer (London: Oxford University Press, 1968), p. 104.
[9] Ibid.
[10] Brian Friel, *Lovers* (Oldcastle: Gallery Press, 1984), p. 11.
[11] The term 'counterfictions' is that of Helen Lojek in 'Brian Friel's Plays and George Steiner's Linguistics: Translating the Irish', *Contemporary Literature*, 35.1 (1994), 83-99, (p. 87).
[12] Brian Friel, *The Loves of Cass McGuire* (Oldcastle: Gallery, 1984), 64.
[13] Ibid, n.p.
[14] Terence Brown, *Ireland: a Social and Cultural History 1922-2002* (London, Harper Perennial, 2nd ed., 2004), p. 356.
[15] Brian Friel, *Plays 2* (London: Faber & Faber, 1999), p. 74. All further references to this text are given in parentheses.
[16] There does not seem to be a stage direction for Michael's exit before the dance scene, but in all the productions I have seen he is absent from it.

NICHOLAS GRENE *is Professor of English Literature at Trinity College Dublin, a Fellow of the College and a Member of the Royal Irish Academy. His books include* The Politics of Irish Drama *(Cambridge University Press, 1999),* Shakespeare's Serial History Plays *(Cambridge University Press, 2002) and* Yeats's Poetic Codes *(Oxford University Press, 2008). He was the founder Director of the Synge Summer School (1991-2000), and chairs the Irish Theatrical Diaspora research network, for which he has edited* Irish Theatre on Tour, *with Chris Morash (Carysfort Press, 2005) and* Interactions: Dublin Theatre Festival 1957-2007 *with Patrick Lonergan (Carysfort Press, 2008). He will be Visiting Professor at the University of Paris-Sorbonne in the spring 2009.*

Irish Theatre International, Vol. 2, No. 1, pp. 48-61

# Space in *Wonderful Tennessee*

Helen Lojek

*Brian Friel's most familiar plays are generally set in indoor space. Often the indoor space is juxtaposed to contiguous exterior space or to fluid, shifting space, but Friel's stages typically present us with enclosed space that suggests norms about who may occupy that space and how they should behave.* Wonderful Tennessee *(1993), however, is set exclusively in exterior space, space that is isolated and to some extent uncontained. Friel uses that exterior setting to situate characters in space less familiar to them and unlikely to play a regular role in their lives. They have sought this space precisely because it frees them from routine, domestic, acceptable order and allows them to search for alternate norms. Friel's use of space—his selection of location and his representation of that location on the stage—underlines the relative vulnerability and freedom of the characters, but also the extent to which actions that occur there constitute an interlude in their lives rather than an on-going reality.*

Brian Friel's most familiar plays are generally set in indoor space. Often the indoor space is juxtaposed to contiguous exterior space or to fluid, shifting space, but Friel's stages typically present us with enclosed space that suggests norms about who may occupy that space and how they should behave. Many of his plays use domestic space: *Philadelphia, Here I Come!* (1964, kitchen, bedroom, and fluid space); *Aristocrats* (1979, interior of Ballybeg Hall and surrounding lawn/garden); *Translations* (1980, home/hedge school interior); *Dancing at Lughnasa* (1990, kitchen interior and surrounding exterior).[1] Even plays that use more public space, like *Freedom of the City* (1973, Mayor's parlour in Derry Guildhall) and *Volunteers* (1975, excavation pits), nevertheless provide audiences with locations that have fixed, acceptable orders. Part of the point of *Freedom of the City*, for example, is precisely that these people should not even be in this space, much less behaving as they are while they are in it. *Wonderful Tennessee* (1993), however, is set exclusively in exterior space, that is isolated and to some extent uncontained. Friel uses that exterior setting to situate characters in space less familiar to them and unlikely to play a regular role in their lives. They have sought this space precisely *because* it frees them from routine, domestic, acceptable order and allows them to search for alternate norms. Friel's use of space — his selection of location and his representation of that location on the stage — underlines the relative vulnerability and freedom of the characters, but also the extent to which actions that occur there constitute an interlude in their lives rather than an on-going reality.

The setting is Ballybeg Pier 'at the end of a headland on the remote coast of northwest Donegal'.[2] Donegal is a liminal area, in the North of Ireland without being in Northern Ireland. For audiences who remember something never mentioned in the play, the fact that the Congested Districts Board (1891-1923) built piers like this along the coast of Donegal, the setting may have very specific resonances.[3] The performances of these characters (aimed at each other as well as at the audience) inhabit an Irish west that has been the site of long-term and largely unsuccessful efforts to create a permanently viable economy. This stone pier retains ample evidence it was once commercially viable, but it is now an abandoned relic, peopled only by six urbanites on a brief excursion. They are far from familiar territory: Trish has difficulty remembering that they are in Donegal (not Sligo), for example, and Frank asserts (despite the evidence around them) that they are 'the first people ever to set foot here.'[4] Terry has optioned the nearby island for which they are headed because he and his sister Trish have childhood memories of it, but those memories are vague and distant and modified by local folklore. For both characters and audience, then, the sense of place in *Wonderful Tennessee* is very different than the sense of place that arrives when a curtain goes up on an Irish kitchen. The opening production at the Abbey Theatre in 1993 emphasized that difference by covering the set with a misty fabric; there was no curtain, and the simulated blowing off of the mist signaled the start of the play.

Seamus Deane has pointed to Donegal's persistence in Friel's imagination as 'a powerful image of possibility, an almost pastoral place in which the principle of hope can find a source.'[5] For Friel's pilgrims, the magical island they have come to visit clearly represents hope, the possibility of a wonderful experience that might salve their broken bodies, uneasy minds, uncertain incomes, and flawed relationships. That hope proves illusory, but it is a temporarily consoling illusion that almost makes life tolerable.

The play's set represents this Donegal territory of hope in ways that allow for the exploration of relationships between human imagination and environment. Like all Friel stage spaces, this one is not a mere framing device, but a powerful representation of the ongoing and complex relationship between humans and their world. The pier stretches the full length of the stage and Friel indicates it is surrounded by water on stage right, on the audience side, and along the back wall. Characters may enter and leave only from stage left. (*Left* and *right* from the perspective of the audience.) This space resembles the sets of *Translations* and *The Communication Cord* in its display of artifacts from an earlier time. It differs from those sets because in *Wonderful Tennessee* none of the 'weather bleached furnishings' have been absorbed by modern life or converted to contemporary use.[6] The feeling is much like that evoked when Frank Hardy, in *Faith Healer*, describes the venues of his healing performances as being littered with 'relics of abandoned rituals'.[7] The remnants of earlier life and use are simply there in *Wonderful Tennessee*, unused, often unrecognized by the visitors, yellow with lichen, rusty, broken. 'The pier was built in 1905 but has not been used since the hinterland became depopulated many decades ago.'[8] Patrick Duffy has described the 'Unprecedented modification of the Irish landscape' by (among other things) new modes of transport.[9] The material and emotional legacy of landscape, he notes, 'are being irreversibly altered'.[10] The built environment of this pier is being slowly reclaimed by the natural environment, but it remains tangible evidence of the impact of humans on landscape, and it gives new meaning to the cliché that Ireland is a 'land of ruins'.

Simultaneously, the relics on Friel's stage are tangible evidences of the abandonment of non-tangible beliefs and traditions. A central feature of the set is a wooden stand, 'cruciform in shape, on which hangs the remnant of a life-belt'.[11] During the play's long opening moments, when no character is on stage, audiences have an opportunity to absorb this visual image — a 'listing and rotting' reminder of two very different sorts of salvation.[12] Friel also specifies that natural sounds be used to convey '*deep tranquillity* [sic] *and peace*'.[13] The sea has a '*gentle heave*'. There is the '*slap and sigh of water against the stone steps*'.[14] Twice Friel notes that the setting is '*idyllic*'.[15] Human sounds begin to invade this idyllic setting, first from off-stage and then when six raucous people enter, clad in bright colours that contrast with the 'weather-bleached' furnishings of the pier, laughing and singing so that '*the idyllic atmosphere is completely shattered*'.[16] In the first two pages of dialogue characters exclaim 'wonderful' six times. They also exclaim 'lost' eleven times and call for 'help' six times. The opening scene, then, establishes disparities that prepare us for central tensions in the drama: rural/urban; contemporary/past; bleached/colorful; idyllic/raucous; physical salvation/spiritual salvation; belief/disbelief; wonderful/lost.

Friel's western Irish space is idyllic, but it is also notable for what is missing from it. Any play set in Ireland is set against the contested spaces of Ireland itself — possessed and disposed; invaded and abandoned; colonized and independent. A play set in the west of Ireland exists against the often common acceptance of artist Paul Henry's notion that to portray the west of Ireland is to reach the 'real soul of Ireland'.[17] In no way, though, does *Wonderful Tennessee*'s portion of the 'authentic' west of Ireland resemble either Henry's notion or the physical and political wilderness once often depicted as uncultivated space full of transgressive, anti-English people and activities (which could be regarded as either threatening or laudable, depending on who was describing them).[18] This portion of the sea side has been transformed by a pier that is no longer useful. The people for whom commercial fishing once provided a living have vanished. Neither colonists nor residents want the area now. Weather, lichen and rot have begun to take the area back, but evidences remain of what Lionel Pilkington has identified as a central concern of Friel's drama: the 'impact of capitalist modernity on traditional society'.[19]

When Friel's urban characters arrive on this Donegal pier, they in part succumb to the power of traditional ritual. They also, however, provide regular reminders of capitalist modernity. Angela and Terry whimsically imagine the island as a 'new venue for rock concerts, wrestling matches [...] Bull fights, revivalist meetings.'[20] George, we are reminded, gave up performing Beethoven sonatas with the 'Aeolians' in order to join the touring 'Dude Ranchers' (who presumably play Irish country and western)[21] and make enough money to get married.[22] Terry remembers his father 'filling a bottle with holy water [on the island] and stuffing the neck with grass'.[23] Terry does not make it to the island on this trip, but he fills a bottle with what he jokingly refers to as 'holy water' (rainwater from a hollow in the pier that he uses to cut the whiskey and refill the brandy bottle) and corks the neck with paper tissues.[24] Friel keeps the capitalist-traditional contrast, and the play provides another example of what Christopher Murray has described as Friel's habit of providing a 'strong social critique by way of [...] some ritualistic action'.[25]

Friel's characters, dropped off by a minibus following a four hour drive, anticipate the arrival of a local resident whose boat will take them to the deserted island, which Terry has optioned as a sort of birthday present to himself. Fortified by drink and supplied with hampers that contain no water but are full of inappropriate food (marrons glacés, brandied peaches, Romanian truffles, and the like), the three couples anticipate not only a birthday celebration but also something wonderful. Determinedly, they sing 'happy' songs, though the lyrics provide a decidedly mixed message. 'O Mother, I could weep for mirth'.[26] 'I want to be happy, but I won't be happy/'Till I make you happy too'.[27] 'When skies are grey and you say you are blue/I'll send the sun shining through'.[28] What they are expressing is not happiness, but a desire *to be* happy. Only the hymns of a religion to which they are clearly no longer firmly committed may hold out genuine hope of happiness. That, however, is not a happiness of this world, and belief in it is difficult. Revealingly, when George first plays 'Regina Caeli' he breaks off mid-phrase. In English, the lyrics are:

> O Queen of heaven, rejoice
> For He whom thou didst merit to bear
>     [*George breaks off.*]
> Hath arisen as He said.
> Pray for us to God.

George has broken off before the lines that express the essence of the Christian faith.[29] Later, in response to Trish's request that he 'Play something exhilarating', George plays 'Regina Caeli' right through, and it is hard not to see in Friel's use of these lines an indication of the crisis of faith that these characters continue to undergo.[30]

Audience members can see neither the countryside nor the sea that surrounds the pier. At the opening curtain they could hear the sounds of the sea, but now all they see is the built environment and all they hear is human voices. Characters, however, can see beyond the pier. Looking over it — 'Next parish Boston, folks!' — and sometimes mounting the catwalk that rises above it, they describe what they see.[31] What they are *looking for* is the magical island that is their hoped-for destination, Oileán Draíochta (Island of Otherness; Island of Mystery). What they *see* is a destination that may be 'no distance out' or 'miles away'; that may have bushes or simply be swathed in clouds; that may be either 'not big' or 'huge'; that may resemble a 'ukulele' or a circle or a rectangle.[32] Characters variously describe it as 'shimmering' like a 'mirage' and as 'spooky'.[33] This shape-shifting island that audiences see only through the eyes of the characters represents that always wished for, but never achieved, wonderful otherness. The ferryman they expect to take them there is as elusive as Godot—or as the 'long-delayed but always expected something that we live for' represented by the Gentleman Caller in Tennessee Williams' *The Glass Menagerie* (1944).[34] There may (or may not) be a hut where he lives just at the edge of the water, and smoke comes from its chimney with inexplicable irregularly. The complex uncertainty of the conflicting descriptions would be impossible if audiences could actually see the island and thus determine its shape for themselves. The descriptions also have a different effect than those in *The Playboy of the Western World*. When Synge's characters gaze out the window to see the mule race that audiences cannot see, the characters all see the same thing and audiences know that Christy has won. The uncertain descriptions of Oileán Draíochta in *Wonderful Tennessee* parallel the conflicting descriptions of the child's birth and death in *Faith Healer*, the Friel play most similar to *Wonderful Tennessee* in its exploration of faith, ceremony, and possible redemption. Audiences do not know what is 'true', and the ambiguity of the descriptions is essential to both plays' explorations of faith. In both plays the ambiguity is facilitated by stage space that provides no 'reality' against which audiences may measure the characters' descriptions. Friel's original title for *Wonderful Tennessee* — *The Imagined Place* — emphasizes the illusory nature of the mystery the characters hope to find on the island. [35]

The set of *Wonderful Tennessee* requires open space that allows for considerable physicality, such as the characters' entrance in a 'clownish, parodic conga dance' with 'a hint of the maenadic.'[36] That dance is worth comparing to the sisters' dance in *Dancing at Lughnasa*.[37] Friel also specifies, though, that these friends *'deposit their belongings at various places along the pier — that place becomes that person's "territory" for the rest of the night.'*[38] The claiming of individual space in the midst of general, open space that 'belongs' to no one is similar to what happens in Frank McGuinness's *Observe the Sons of Ulster Marching Towards the Somme* (1985) when the soldiers spread their bedrolls out on the ground. In both plays, this use of space allows characters both to come together in song or play and to 'drift apart'[39] into pairs or solitude, sometimes retreating into individual privacies — to be, as most humans are, both communal and individual.[40] Visually, then, Friel's use of unconfined, undomesticated exterior space provides images of the ways in which individuals are both drawn together and drawn apart. They seek comfort both in community and in privacy, but neither community nor privacy is always comforting. These friends and relatives can and do hurt each other when they come together, and their privacies are often painful and lonely. The use of the stage space allows audiences to see as well as hear these complexities.

The ferryman for whom they wait has been there 'for generations', part of a ferrying tradition that has existed 'for thousands of years'.[41] He is described in ways that clearly associate him with Charon, the ancient Greek charged with ferrying the souls of the dead across the river Styx, transporting them from the world of the living to the world of the dead. Friel's ferryman, whose name is Carlin, is 'Ancient; and filthy; and toothless. And bloody smiling all the time.'[42] The dialogue is littered with classical references that make it difficult to avoid the Charon/Carlin connection, but there is no indication the characters see their island destination as a world of the dead in any negative sense. If it is a world of the dead, it is also a world of holy otherness, a sort of salvation.

Angela, a classics instructor, has the most extensive knowledge of Greek mythology, but all of the characters are comfortable with the images, which pervade their contemporary Irish world and offer an allusive alternative to it. (Greek and Latin language and mythology play a similar role in *Translations*.) They

hope, for example, to see dolphins, an invariably positive force in Greek mythology, representing friendship, joy, harmony, health, and safe travels (including
travels to another world). Frank claims to have seen a dolphin, but his camera is
out of film and so he cannot photograph it.[43] He has also lied earlier about seeing Carlin, so his credibility in general is suspect. Like the island itself, the dolphins remain just beyond range of a clear or permanent view.

 References to Greek religion are mingled with a host of reminders of
other faiths: Angela's name, her parody of an American evangelist, various Christian hymns, Berna(dette)'s full name, references to the 1932 Eucharistic Congress
in Dublin and to the young people who left that Congress in an excited (spiritual?
emotional? demonic?) state that led to the ritualistic slaying and dismemberment
of a comrade.[44] That parodic sacrifice took place on Oileán Draíochta, which has
also been the location of a Middle Age church dedicated to Saint Conall, of pil-
grimages seeking healing by a holy well, and of *poitín* manufacture and drunken
orgies. Frank declares that 'People stopped believing, didn't they?',[45] and the
signs of unstable belief are everywhere, as for instance in the fact that Berna pro-
claims 'Lord, it is good for us to be here!' while mounted on a rotten fish-box.[46] A
more general problem is the difficulty of knowing what to believe in. The jumble
of religious references, the Donegal setting, the centrality of the cruciform wooden
stand — all emphasize the play's space as a space of hope (however tattered) and
directly reflect Friel's assessment that this play deals with 'the necessity for mystery. It's mystery, not religion, but mystery finds its expression in this society
mostly in religious practice.'[47] The stage space also emphasizes the fact that hope
and mystery are always elsewhere — on an island that cannot be reached, or in
Tennessee, where none of the characters has been or wants to go.

 Friel's title comes from 'Down by the Cane-brake', a song Terry and Trish
remember hearing their mother sing. (They recall their father singing 'I Don't
Know Why I'm Happy'.) When Terry asks 'What's a cane-brake?' Angela responds 'Shelter-belt of canes, I suppose. Protection against the elements.'[48] Angela is correct to an extent, though canebrakes, which occur in swampy areas, are
more likely to shelter animals than humans. More significant implications are ev
ident in Friel's report that he used 'Down by the Cane-brake' 'because it was a
song my mother sang; and because the words of the song — the promise of happiness in the Eden of Tennessee — those words echo the theme of the play'.[49] The
'Eden of Tennessee' — Wonderful Tennessee — holds out the promise (not nec-
essarily the reality) of happiness. Like the island of wonder, it is elusive and perhaps illusive. Terry sees Angela, whom he has loved and lost, looking through
the binoculars and asks 'Tennessee still there?' Angela replies 'Lost it again', to
which Terry responds 'Still there. "Believe me."'[50] Like 'wonderful', the word 'belief' echoes throughout the play. But wonderful things that warrant belief remain
distant and elsewhere. Possible answers to the question of why a play set in west
Donegal bears the name of one of the United States emerge only gradually, and
the song title is both relevant and misleadingly narrow. The sound of *Tennessee*
links it to *sea* (ocean) and *see* (vision). *Wonderful* is rooted in *wonder* (religious
awe and ecstasy but also questioning and curiosity). The song is repeated in a
variety of contexts in Friel's play, so that wonder is vested in Tennessee, in mar-

riage, and in heaven. Both song and play associate wonder and freedom not just
with water, but also with the past.

Robert Tracy has pointed out that Friel revised the original minstrel
lyrics, changing Nancy from 'a colored gal' to 'a blue-eyed girl' — thus eliminat-
ing the specifically African-American yearnings it represented.[51] There may also
be an echo of an event John Hildebidle told me about in 1994: Apparently shortly
before *Wonderful Tennessee* was completed, Friel's friend and colleague Seamus
Heaney had been in Tennessee and had almost but not quite made it to Elvis Pres-
ley's Graceland, the Memphis (Tennessee) mansion whose name echoes concerns
in Friel's play. Heaney's trip (and Paul Simon's vision in 'Goin' to Graceland')
may be floating in the background of this play's title. And Friel is undoubtedly
aware of the large number of Irish (particularly Ulster Irish) who settled in Tennessee, preserving in exile part of their cultural ties with Ireland.[52] The multi-
plicity of possible echoes, a device typical of Friel's work, makes the title more
ambiguous and more culturally diverse than it might seem at first glance — and
a far less specifically geographic place reference.

It is also possible that the play's title contains an allusion to Tennessee
Williams, a playwright mentioned relatively infrequently by Friel, but always with
awareness of contrasts and connections between his own plays and those of the
American playwright.[53] Friel's urban characters, gathered on the west coast and
looking toward an island of otherness whose significance is as much imagined as
historical, are positioned in space in ways parallel to the space occupied by major
characters in Williams' plays. Amanda Wingfield (*The Glass Menagerie*, 1944),
surrounded by the discordant urban realities of St. Louis, remembers her southern origins on Blue Mountain, where life and love were easier — a romantic vision
of a kind of sacred otherness, an awareness of exile and of a place that is no longer
reachable.[54] Her husband and her son escape geographically. Her daughter escapes into fantasy. In Williams' *A Streetcar named Desire* (1947), Blanche
DuBois' arrival in New Orleans does not displace her yearning for Belle Rive, the
beautiful dream of a plantation where she imagines life was better and from which
she is now permanently exiled. She (like Friel's Berna?) escapes into madness. In
both Williams's plays, the imagined other places (like Oileán Draíochta in *Wonderful Tennessee* and like Yolland's romantic image of Celtic Ireland in *Translations*) represent alternatives to modern urbanism, but they are unreal,
unreachable, and associated with the past. Like Williams' characters, Friel's seek
a place where reality is more bearable, and where they have a place. Like
Williams's characters, Friel's will never reach such a place because it is imagined
and illusory — one reason it is always associated with the past. For both playwrights, though, these imagined places are key elements in our understanding of
the play's focus on the necessary mystery lacking in present reality.

Friel's use of American place names in the titles of *Wonderful Tennessee*
and *Philadelphia, Here I Come!* expands the resonances of place in both works.
In *Philadelphia*, Gar imagines that the American city will allow him access to a
fuller, richer life. He imagines this despite ample evidence to the contrary, and
Philadelphia becomes an imagined other to the constrictions of Balleybeg. Gar actually goes to Philadelphia, though it is doubtful he will find the city he has imag-

ined. Characters in *Wonderful Tennessee* will never go to Tennessee, any more than they will ever reach Oiléan Draíochta. Tennessee, in fact, may be wonderful precisely *because* the glorious alternative it offers to Irish places will never be diminished by direct experience. It will never be reality in the way Ireland is reality. The main function of Friel's title references to America has shifted: Philadelphia was a place of hope to be reached; Tennessee is a place of hope precisely because it will remain out of reach and thus wonderful.

For decades Friel has lamented Ireland's transformation into 'a tenth rate image of America',[55] describing the island as 'a shabby imitation of a third-rate American state'.[56] 'We [the Irish] think that exile is miserable', he has said, and the childlessness of his Irish-American characters reflects his sense of the sterility of American culture. [57] America has long, however, represented for the Irish not only the necessity of immigration, but also the hope of immigration. *Philadelphia* reflects both the necessity and the hope. *Wonderful Tennessee* projects an illusory hope and links it to an illusory place. It all but deliberately reverses the substance of the biblical sentiment that 'faith is the substance of things hoped for, the evidence of things not seen' (Hebrews, 11:1) and presents a more fatalistic view of Irish life.

Partrick Mason, who directed the original production, has observed that 'Ultimately, the last ten minutes of the play is about a sacred space ... Ritual is something you undergo, not something you talk about'.[58] Friel's stage space allows for a closing that is as visual as his opening, with each character participating in a ritual encircling movement that includes lifting a stone and placing a votive offering on the cruciform stand. There is music, but the ritual is otherwise wordless — an extended, powerful, sacred action. On the other hand, the ritual began as a game, and when it is concluded and the characters have left the stage, audiences are left with an unsettling image: The cruciform lifebelt stand that was the focus of the opening has been draped with 'votive offerings': a hat on top, a belt around the middle, a bracelet and scarf on the arms.[59] It resembles a person — or perhaps just a scarecrow.

Mason reported that at the end of the thirteen week Dublin run but before the Broadway opening, Friel felt the need for a more affirmative ending to the play and added a few lines.[60] Originally, George (who is dying) and Angela were left alone on the stage, the final participants in the ritual completed by the others, who have left for the minibus that will take them home. George asks Angela to come back to the pier some day 'in memory of me', and Angela promises to come back 'For both of us!' They leave singing 'Down by the Cane-brake', the bus's engine starts, and gradually silence takes over, leaving the space almost as it was in the opening scene.[61] Between the Dublin and Broadway productions, Friel slightly expanded Angela's closing response to George:

> Yes, George, I will. Some day, yes. Not in deference. I'm damned if I'll live there. But for you. Happily, happily for you, brave man. For both of us. Until I come back.[lxii]

The addition increases the affirmation of the ending, but only slightly, and the bleakness of the end is linked to the play's use of space.

The entire play has been spent in waiting for Carlin/Charon to ferry these friends to the Island of Mystery that may also be the Island of the Dead. He does not come, and they cannot reach the island. At the end, Charlie comes back with the minibus to take them home. Charlie's name also echoes Charon, a point Friel emphasizes by having characters confuse the names Carlin and Charlie three times.[63] Frank notes that 'At seven-thirty in the morning the rage for the absolute isn't quite so consuming ... The acceptance of what *is* ...',[64] but he does not finish his sentence, and while the friends seem initially *'joyous'* at the arrival of the minibus, their excitement gradually dies away.[65] Is the city a less wonderful, less mysterious place of the dead, at least metaphorically, to which a different Charon not only *can* but also *does* transport them? In Greek mythology, souls who do not have a coin to pay for passage to the world of the dead are doomed to wander the banks of the River Styx forever. Is that what has happened to Friel's characters? Are they doomed to wander? Or have they merely made a pragmatic decision to give up the elusive possibility of happiness in order to get on with the realities of life? Why does George want Angela to come back to the pier, where they have hardly spent a lovely evening, despite the marvellous concluding ceremony? Is it the pier he wants her to return to? Is he hoping that a return to the pier will provide access to the island? Or does this dying man just hope to be remembered in connection with the Island of Otherness? Answers to such questions are as mysterious as the island itself. Richard Allen Cave has noted that Friel 'pursues a delicate line of enquiry into the nature and function of ritual in contemporary life', but it is not an enquiry that reaches any clear or firm conclusions.[66]

Despite their evident longing for the timelessness of myth and ritual, these friends are very much in time. Frank's projected book is *The Measurement of Time and Its Effect on European Civilization*.[67] Berna's watch stops when she jumps in the sea, and she throws it away.[68] Frank refers to the insistence that Terry leave a votive offering as 'killing time [...] a bit of fun', a phrase that brings to mind the injunction that it is impossible to kill time without injuring eternity.[69] The expedition as a whole has time constraints that the friends constantly discuss: Will Carlin come soon enough to get them to the island and back on time? When will Charlie return with the minibus? How long will George live? At best, their time in Donegal will constitute what Friel (echoing the words Robert Frost used of poetry) described as the power of 'sacred song, [which is] the only momentary stay we have against confusion'.[70]

Space, as well as time, reinforces the challenge of the situation in which these characters find themselves and reveals the narrowness of their choices. On a pier surrounded on three sides by water, characters may enter and exit only to the left, the area from which we hear the noise of that modern day ferry, the minibus. They cannot get to the island without the ferryman who does not arrive. They cannot stay longer in the borderland where they have spent the night. Their only real option is to climb back on the minibus and return to the lives (and impending deaths) from which they have temporarily escaped. These realities are clear in the dialogue, but also in the physical space of the play—space that manages to be incredibly confining despite its lack of walls.

Reviewing the first production of *Wonderful Tennessee*, Fintan O'Toole noted Friel's on-going struggle 'with the idea of faith, with the pull between the chaos of life and the intimations of the inexpressible that surround it'.[71] O'Toole, who did not particularly like the play, complained that Friel's borrowings from classical literature and imagery were never 'reimagined and transformed' and that Friel had not managed to imbue the ordinary with the mythic, leaving 'the mythic ... reduced to a very ordinary dullness'.[72] 'Removing his characters from society', O'Toole concluded is the ultimate attempt to throw off the shackles of Irish complication.[73] But without the weight of a wider world pressing on his characters' lives, they come to seem ... insignificant and curiously weightless. Typically, O'Toole has put his cursor on central dramatic issues. The ordinary dullness of the mythic with which Friel leaves audiences, however, may be his intent, and certainly that impact is underscored by his use of stage space.

Friel's characters may indeed have shuffled off the weight of a wider world that includes impending death by cancer, mental illness, tense marital relationships, and the probable bankruptcy of the promoter/bookie/gambler who has been the chief support of all three couples. They have not, however, all arrived on the pier expecting or even hoping to be transformed by the mythic. The stage space is incredibly narrow, and those key moments of the play that are performed without dialogue (the early conga dance; the closing ritual; the music) must be performed in constricted space.[74] Characters may not exit stage right because Carlin has not arrived to ferry them to the island. They entered stage left, and they will exit in that direction, but only when Charlie has returned to minibus them back to the city. Their movements are constricted by a literal and metaphoric space that leaves them few options other than to dance slightly left and slightly right, or to mount temporarily to the cat-walk from which they may (perhaps) see the Island of Otherness. They know what lies stage left—the 'wider world' that has not presented them with the lives they seem to want. They are not sure what lies stage right, but it represents a mythic otherness that they will give only a brief opportunity to transform them. Is Carlin the ferryman a modern Charon? Or is Charlie the minibus driver Charon's reincarnation? Do they really want to be transported to Oileán Draíochta, or would they prefer being transported back to modern urban life? If Charon does not arrive, will they (like Greek souls without the coin to pay Charon) be left wandering the banks of the Styx, lost souls never saved? Is Hades stage right? Stage left? Or center stage? And where in the world (or out of it) is Heaven?

The ritual these couples engage in before they depart echoes one Terry remembers from a childhood visit to the island.[75] It may seem initially to reclaim mythic traditions, and Friel has worked hard to provide a gleam of optimism in Angela's promise to return. Ultimately, though, the conclusion is overwhelmingly ambivalent. By limiting themselves to a brief ritual and returning to their mundane lives, the characters simultaneously praise and condemn ritual, ignoring the value of ritual even as they appear to notice and engage in it. They have not been able to escape the narrow spaces of their lives any more than they have been able to find a desirable way off the pier or to manoeuver extensively on the narrow stage space. Their 'escape' from urban modernity has been temporary, and their attempt to reclaim the power of myth is doomed because they are never able to relocate mythic understandings into their own world. The contemporary world has shaped other modes of understanding, and the effort to reclaim and translate mythic understandings is as futile as the effort to resist the mapmaking and translation in *Translations*.

In the essays, diaries, and interviews that Christopher Murray has collected, Friel makes regular references to T.S. Eliot.[76] In *Wonderful Tennessee*, Frank has lines that echo lines in Eliot's 'The Love Song of J. Alfred Prufrock': Our most important desires, Frank says are 'inexpressible ... ineffable'. Before them 'language stands baffled' and 'says of what it has attempted to say, "No, no! That's not it at all! No, not at all!"' Friel's keen awareness of the limits of language is part of the impetus for his rich ambiguity, which illustrates his refusal to simplify in order to express, and his emphasis on the visual as well as the verbal. For me, the feeling at the end of *Wonderful Tennessee* parallels the feeling in the final lines of 'Prufrock':

> I have heard the mermaids singing, each to each.
> I do not think that they will sing to me.

On this Donegal pier, six individuals look for an island and dolphins. They are nostalgic for what they imagine those things represent. Ultimately, though, the Island of Otherness is unreachable. Like the elusive happiness Berna has earlier described, it is 'the real thing *almost* within grasp, just a step away. Maybe that's the norm'.[77] As Friel put it in a programme note for Tom Murphy's *The Blue Macushla* (1980), 'The only constant in life is the yearning for something that must be better than what is. The only certainty is that that yearning can never be satisfied'.[78]

Friel's return in *Wonderful Tennessee* to his familiar territory of Donegal, and the representation of that territory on stage provide audiences with powerful visual images of the narrow range within which people must operate in hopes of grasping not only elusive happiness, but also mythic beliefs that will enrich their lives. Like the play itself, though, the trip to Donegal is only a momentary stay against the confusions of life.

## NOTES

[1] Other examples include *The Loves of Cass McGuire* (1966, living room and common room); *Faith Healer* (1979, sparsely represented interior of a public hall); *Living Quarters* (1982, living room and garden of the family home); *The Communication Cord* (1982, kitchen of an updated 'traditional' Irish cottage); *Give Me Your Answer, Do!* (1997, interior and surrounding lawn/garden).

[2] Brian Friel, *Wonderful Tennessee* (County Meath: Gallery, 1993), p. 8.

[3] The CDB (established by Britain's 1891 Land Act and operating until 1923) also supported railroads, roads, carpet making, and boats.

[4] *Wonderful Tennessee*, I. i. p. 13.

[5] Seamus Deane 'Introduction' in *Selected Plays Brian Friel* (London & Boston: Faber and Faber Ltd., 1984), p. 11-12.

[6] *Wonderful Tennessee*, p. 8.

[7] Brian Friel, *Faith Healer* (Co. Meath: Gallery Books, 1991), p. 12.

[8] *Wonderful Tennessee*, p. 8.

[9] *Wonderful Tennessee*, I. i. p. 13.

[10] Patrick J. Duffy, *Exploring the History and Heritage of Irish Landscape* (Dublin: Four Courts, 2007), p. 13.

[11] *Wonderful Tennessee*, p. 8.

[12] Ibid.

[13] *Wonderful Tennessee*, I. i. p. 11.

[14] Ibid.

[15] *Wonderful Tennessee*, I. i. p. 11.

[16] Ibid.

[17] Quoted in S.B.Kennedy, *Paul Henry: Paintings, Drawings, Illustrations* (New Haven: Yale UP, 1999), p. 84.

[18] Csilla Bertha has analyzed Friel's simultaneous evocation and inversion of the unspoiled natural setting common in nineteenth-century melodramas about Ireland. 'Six Characters in Search of a Faith: *Wonderful Tennessee*' *Irish University Review* 29.1(Spring/Summer 1999), pp. 119-35.

[19] Lionel Pilkington, 'Reading History in the Plays of Brian Friel' in *A Companion to Modern British and Irish Drama (1880-2005)* ed. Mary Luckhurst (Oxford UK: Blackwell, 2006), p. 499.

[20] *Wonderful Tennessee*, I. i. p. 38.

[21] Michael Robinson, who once played Beethoven sonatas with George, is now down and out in London (I. i. p. 37). Trish has earlier referred to this area as 'Bloody Indian territory'(I. i. p.19), and *Wonderful Tennessee* shares with other Friel scripts a tendency to invoke terms associated with the US west.

[22] *Wonderful Tennessee*, I. ii. pp. 62-3.

[23] *Wonderful Tennessee*, I. i. p. 30.

[24] *Wonderful Tennessee*, II. p. 78.

[25] Christopher Murray 'Introduction' in *Brian Friel: Essays, Diaries, Interviews: 1964-1999* (London & New York: Faber and Faber Ltd., 1999), p. xvi.

[26] *Wonderful Tennessee*, I. i. p. 12.

[27] *Wonderful Tennessee*, I. i. p. 13.

[28] *Wonderful Tennessee*, I. i. pp. 14-5.

[29] *Wonderful Tennessee*, I. ii. p. 47.

[30] *Wonderful Tennessee*, II. p. 67.

[31] *Wonderful Tennessee*, I. i. p. 9.

[32] *Wonderful Tennessee*, I. i. pp. 27-30.

[33] Ibid.

[34] Tennessee Williams, *The Glass Menagerie* ( NY: New Directions, 1970), p. 23.

[35] Brian Friel, Interview with Mel Gussow (1991). Reprinted in Murray, *op.cit.*, p. 148. Friel's use of "Imagined Place" is worth comparing to the tradition explored by Janice Hewlett Koelb in *The Poetics of Description: Imagined Places in European Literature* (Palgrave, 2006). Koelb explains the classical practice of *ecphrasis* as a "notion of vividness that makes imaginative eyewitnesses of the audience" (p. 1) and explores *ecphrasis* in European (largely nineteenth century) literature as a way of creating images not only for memory, but also for creative perception.

[36] *Wonderful Tennessee*, I. i. p. 17.

[37] For an informative discussion of the play's physicality, see Richard Allen Cave, 'Questing for Ritual and Ceremony in a Godforsaken World: *Dancing at Lughnasa* and *Wonderful Tennessee*'. In *Brian Friel's Dramatic Artistry: 'The Work Has Value'* ed. by

Donald E. Morse, Csilla Bertha and Mária Kurdi (Dublin: Carysfort, 2006), pp. 181-204. José Lanters has examined the effect of the characters' deliberate, self-conscious performances, which often approach parody. 'Violence and Sacrifice in Brian Friel's *The Gentle Island* and *Wonderful Tennessee*', *Irish University Review* 26.1 (1996), p. 175.

[38] *Wonderful Tennessee*, I. i. p. 19.

[39] *Wonderful Tennessee*, I. i. p. 36.

[40] *Wonderful Tennessee*, I. ii. p. 40.

[41] *Wonderful Tennessee*, I. i. pp. 34-5.

[42] *Wonderful Tennessee*, I. ii. p. 42.

[43] *Wonderful Tennessee*, II. p. 70.

[44] A similar jumble of ancient ritual, modern drunkenness, and dangerous consequences appears during festival time in *Dancing at Lughnasa*.

[45] *Wonderful Tennessee*, I. i. p. 31.

[46] *Wonderful Tennessee*, I. i. p. 38.

[47] Interview with Mel Gussow. *op. cit.* 148.

[48] *Wonderful Tennessee*, I. ii. p. 41.

[49] Notes for the Friel Festival programme (1999). Reprinted in Murray, *op. cit.*, p. 176-77.

[50] *Wonderful Tennessee*, I. ii. p. 46.

[51] "Work in Progress." Review of Wonderful Tennessee. *The Irish Literary Supplement.* Spring 1992, pp. 17-18.

[52] See, for example, Billy Kennedy, *The Scots-Irish in the Hills of Tennessee* (Belfast: Causeway Press, 1995).

[53] See, for example, a 1966 interview with John Fairleigh in which Friel observes that 'Tennessee Williams starts off with unbelievable characters and then sets out to make them credible. I use the stock people and then have to make something of them.' 'After *Philadelphia*.' Reprinted in *Brian Friel in Conversation* ed. Paul Delaney (Ann Arbor: U Michigan Press, 2000), pp. 47-50.

[54] Amanda indicates that Blue Mountain is in the Mississippi Delta, which includes western Tennessee — not far from St. Louis, Missouri, where she now lives. Missouri is not part of the American South if by "South" we mean the states of the Confederacy, so Amanda's exile is larger than the geographic distance she has travelled.

[55] Interview with Desmond Rushe (1970). Reprinted in Murray, *op. cit.*, p. 27.

[56] Interview with Des Hickey and Gus Smith (1972). Reprinted in Murray, *op. cit.* 49.

[57] Interview with Fintan O'Toole (1982). Reprinted in Murray, *op. cit.*, p. 112.

[58] In *From Ballybeg to Broadway*. Dir: Donald Taylor Black. A Ferndale Films Production for RTE and BBC Northern Ireland. 1994.

[59] *Wonderful Tennessee*, II. p. 89.

[60] Mason quoted in *From Ballybeg to Broadway*.

[61] *Wonderful Tennessee*, II. pp. 89-90.

[62] Ibid.

[63] *Wonderful Tennessee*, I. ii. p. 56 and II. p. 83.

[64] *Wonderful Tennessee*, II. p. 82.

[65] *Wonderful Tennessee*, II. pp. 84-5.

[66] Richard Allen Cave, p. 181.

[67] *Wonderful Tennessee*, I. ii. p. 50.

[68] *Wonderful Tennessee*, I. ii. p. 66.

[69] *Wonderful Tennessee*, II. pp. 81-2.

[70] 'Kitezh' in the Friel Festival programme. Reprinted in Murray, *op. cit.*, p. 180. Frost's description of poetry as 'a momentary stay against confusion' came in 'The Figure a Poem Makes' (1938).

[71] 'Wonderful Tennessee' (1993).  Reprinted in *Critical Moments: Fintan O'Toole on Modern Irish Theatre* ed. Julia Furay and Redmond O'Hanlon (Dublin: Carysfort, 2003), p. 112.

[72] *Critical Moments: Fintan O'Toole on Modern Irish Theatre*, p. 114.

[73] *Ibid.*

[74] See, for example, the photograph reprinted in the Friel Festival programme (April-August 1999), p. 24

[75] *Wonderful Tennessee.* I. i. p. 30.

[76] see Murray, *op. cit.*

[77] *Wonderful Tennessee*, I. ii. p. 44.

[78] Reprinted in Murray, *op. cit.*, p. 90.

HELEN LOJEK *is Professor of English and Associate Dean, College of Arts and Sciences, at Boise State University, Idaho, where she teaches American literature and contemporary English language drama. Articles on Brian Friel, Frank McGuinness, Anne Devlin and the Charabanc Theatre Company have appeared in such journals as* Contemporary Literature, Modern Drama, *and* Irish University Review. *Her books include* The Theatre of Frank McGuinness: Stages of Mutability *(Dublin: Carysfort, 2002) and* Contexts for Frank McGuinness's Drama *(Washington, D.C.: Catholic University Press, 2004).*

Irish Theatre International, Vol. 2, No. 1, pp. 62-68

## *The Home Place*: Unhomely Inheritances

Anna McMullan

*Brian Friel's* The Home Place *premiered at the Dublin Gate Theatre in February 2005, directed by Adrian Noble. In Friel's 80th year, 2009, the play was directed by Mick Gordon, and produced by the Lyric Theatre at the Grand Opera House in Belfast. This article is concerned with the unsettling, dislocated quality of* The Home Place *in performance, and especially, in the juxtaposition of moments of 'crude' theatricality with the haunting off-stage voices of children singing Thomas Moore's 'Oft in the Stilly Night'. To what extent is Friel using theatrical conventions, and particularly on and off stage, appearances and disappearances, to raise questions about inheritances imposed or lost, and related questions of possession and dispossession, home and displacement?*

Brian Friel's *The Home Place* premiered at the Dublin Gate Theatre in February 2005, directed by Adrian Noble. It is, at writing, Friel's latest play, following *Performances* (2003) which explored the life and work of Czech composer Leos Janacek, and incorporates a performance of his final string quartet, *Intimate Letters*. *The Home Place* returns to Ballybeg, and to a big house, though this time (and the first in Friel's canon), it belongs to an Anglo-Irish landlord in the late nineteenth century. In Friel's 80th year, 2009, the play was directed by Mick Gordon, and produced by the Lyric Theatre at the Grand Opera House in Belfast. While both productions received acclaim, there were some critical reservations. A review in *Variety* of the 2005 production acknowledged the global resonance of Friel's play, while complaining that dramatically it 'doesn't quite hit home'.[1] In 2009, Jane Coyle referred to the play as 'bewitching' but commented that, despite 'high profile casting and excellent production values', characters appeared 'stranded and detached'.[2] I am interested in the unsettling, dislocated quality of *The Home Place* in performance, and especially, in the juxtaposition of moments of 'crude' theatricality with the haunting off-stage voices of children singing Thomas Moore's 'Oft in the Stilly Night'. To what extent is Friel using theatrical conventions, and particularly on and off stage, appearances and disappearances, to raise questions about inheritances imposed or lost, and related questions of possession and dispossession, home and displacement?

The term 'unhomely' derives originally from Freud's *unheimlich*, which he defines as the recurrence of the once familiar which has become 'uncanny and frightening', as the long ago repressed of the individual or cultural psyche returns to haunt the present.[3] The post-colonial critic Homi Bhabha takes up this concept of the uncanny in *The Location of Culture*, and renames it the 'unhomely'. He explores how the legacies or hauntings of history disrupt the present in such texts as Toni Morrison's novel, *Beloved*.[4] They indicate an unresolved trauma, a lost legacy with which the present must come to terms. Jacques Derrida has written about the haunting of history in *Spectres of Marx* and *Echographies of Television* as an active injunction to the present to sift through our diverse legacies: 'An inheritance is never gathered together, it is never one with itself. Its presumed unity, if there is one, can consist only in the *injunction* to *reaffirm by choosing'* [italics in original].[5] In the nineteenth century setting of *The Home Place*, Margaret O'Donnell is faced with such a choice, which resonates in contemporary Ireland and especially contemporary Northern Ireland, over a hundred years later.

The set for *The Home Place* recalls Chekhov's *The Cherry Orchard* in its depiction of a house surrounded by trees, some of which, though not all, are hewn down at the end of the play. It is set in 1878, which as several critics note, was a period on the threshold of change. The local resistance organized by Con Doherty will develop into the Land Wars, the foundation of the Land League and the rise of Parnell. Scott Boltwood comments: 'Friel deliberately chooses to depict the Protestant aristocracy in the last days before its power was deliberately challenged'.[6] The play uses the late nineteenth century theatrical conventions of naturalism, with recognizable characters as metonyms of a social structure, and a set that suggests a particular time and place. A large section of the social structure of Ballybeg appears on or off stage, and everyone is displaced.

The set remains unchanged during the play. The audience sees only the breakfast room of the house, which opens onto an 'unkempt' lawn. The traffic between interior and exterior and between on and off stage maintains a focus on thresholds and transit.[7] As indicated in the script, the Grand Opera House production opened silently with the two women of the household working: the housekeeper Margaret folds washing on the lawn, the maid works at the fire in the house, their activities, costume and relation to the space all indicating their social position in the layered social structures of Ballybeg. Throughout the play Margaret is careful to align herself with the Gores, rather than with the locals. She is distant to Con Doherty, and is unhappy to be reminded that he is a cousin of hers. When her inebriated father appears later in act one, she is ashamed of him, and tries to dispatch him: 'You'll get no drink in this house. Off you go now!'[8] However, when she hears the children's voices from the schoolhouse, Margaret is drawn, almost pulled, to the front edge of the stage as the memories of her past possess her, as in the Thomas Moore song she is listening to: 'Sad memory brings the light / of other days around me'.[9] Indeed Margaret is not only caught between home places, but generations, as she is courted by both Christopher Gore, and his son David.

On the morning that the play opens, Christopher Gore has attended the funeral of a particularly exploitative and brutal neighbour, Lord Lifford: he was attacked and killed by local militants. We gradually realize that this militant resistance to exploitative local landlords is being led by Con, who is courting Sally the maid, and who has returned from meetings in London. If Ireland of the early twenty-first century was declared the most globalized country on earth,[10] *The Home Place* emphasizes the displacements of empire and resistance that made of Ireland a global network centuries previously.[11] Christopher Gore cites Kent as his home place: his sense of exile intensifies during the play, and indeed he always seems to be coming and going in and out of the house (named The Lodge). David refers first to Glasgow and then to extended family in Kenya as possible places that he could make a new life with Margaret, who indeed returns his love, but is sceptical of his unrealistic plans.

Into this already unsettled social network, enters Christopher's brother Dr Richard Gore, and his assistant, Perkins (from the Norfolk Fens). Gore is an ardent anthropologist and craniologist (Margaret and Christopher argue over the correct terminology) and he has come to Ireland to measure the natives. This was indeed a mania at the turn of the century and part of the Victorian obsession with classification, particularly racial classification. Anne McClintock suggests that in the Victorian era, the categories of race, class and gender were produced in and through each other as a way not only of maintaining British colonial supremacy, but of domestically policing the '"dangerous classes": the working class, the Irish, Jews, prostitutes, feminists, gays and lesbians, criminals, the militant crowd and so on.'[12] Friel includes an extract from a 1892 lecture given by Professor A. C. Haddon to the Royal Irish Academy on 'Studies in Irish Craniology: The Aran Islands, County Galway'. Richard Gore believes that if 'we', presumably the British ruling class, could master this technique: 'we wouldn't control just an empire. We would rule the entire universe.'[13] Both Richard and Perkins come across as somewhat stereotyped: Dr Gore's attitude of ownership over the locals is played out also in his overtly sexist behaviour to Sally: '(*He slaps her bottom in dismissal.*) Back to the paddock.'[14] In the stage directions, it is suggested that both Richard Gore and Perkins self-consciously perform roles:

> *Richard is a bachelor in his sixties. A man of resolute habits and Victorian confidence: he is aware that this is how he is seen and it gives him sly pleasure to play up to that stereotype. Perkins, his personal assistant, is in his forties. Like his employer, he knows he plays a role; and he, too, enjoys playing it.*[15]

Conleth Hill played up this self-conscious element of masquerade rather more in the Lyric production than Nick Dunning in the original Gate production. It suggested to me, that Friel may have deliberately fashioned elements of 'stereotype' into the character of Dr Gore and indeed, into the second act of the play.

The scene where Richard and Perkins measure the heads of some local peasants is certainly a 'crude' spectacle.[16] Here again, the use of off-stage and thresholds between house and lawn emphasize the displacement of the peasants who are uncomfortable in this environment – except for the '*scampish*' and '*irrepressible*' Tommy Boyle from Lough Anna (a location familiar from *Dancing at Lughnasa*). The off stage lane marks the delimitation of the Lodge and the rest of Ballybeg. An additional spectator however, is Con who has returned with a sinister hitman to end the humiliating proceedings. He refers to several others waiting at the bottom of the lane, including one who he infers has just murdered Lifford (who was found still clutching a lock of his assailant's dark hair). There is no violence on stage, and yet the colonial authority of the measuring scene and the threatened violence of the local vigilantes (though Con insists they 'have no quarrel' with Christopher) make for very uncomfortable viewing. The peasant characters who appear only briefly are difficult not to stereotype. But perhaps the crudeness of this scene echoes the stark legacies of the historical forces represented by these figures. Raymond Williams reminds us that: 'the serious and exploring drama, from Ibsen and Chekhov and Strindberg to Brecht and Beckett, was faced always with a contradiction: that what it seemed to make real, in theatrical terms, was what it wished to show as a limited reality, in dramatic terms.'[17] Friel's introduction of a stereotypical opposition in the imperialist Richard Gore and the vigilante organizers, may have a similar aim of foregrounding the limitation of these options as inheritances.

As a contrast to this spectacle of exploitation and threat, there is a brief anterior scene with Margaret's father, the schoolmaster. He is on stage for only a few minutes, but he offers an alternative mode of gauging both identity and inheritance, through the music of Thomas Moore:

> He has our true measure, Mr Richard. He divines us accurately. He reproduces features of our history and our character. And he is an astute poet who knows that certain kinds of songs are necessary for his people. And they were especially necessary at the time he sang them.[18]

Harry White has written of the role of Moore's music in the play as a kind of home place: 'a mode of identity and refuge' for a politically, culturally and materially dispossessed people.[19] Moore was referred to as the Bard of Erin and Ireland's national poet.[20] Yet, as O'Donnell hints, Thomas Moore was also a complex transnational figure, friend (and biographer) of Lord Bryon, and an important influence on the European Romantic movement in music. But Moore's popularity also led to a dismissal of his legacy. In his study of music and the Irish literary imagination, White charts Moore's 'swift declension from national poet to the embodiment of a popular culture which both the Gaelic League and the Literary Revival quickly disdained'.[21] At the time of the play, Moore's reputation amongst the rising political and cultural players was in decline. Nationalism was suspicious of his British popularity, and promoted political ballads instead. However, White identifies Moore as a careful translator 'from Irish music into English verse',[22] and cites Matthew Campbell on Moore's melodies:

> 'Translation' in the *Melodies* is not from Irish into English, which the lyrics never pretend to do, or even entirely from music into words, but more precisely from the music of one nation into the language of another.[23]

Yet 'Oft in the Stilly Night', the song sung by the children in *The Home Place*, is not from *Irish Melodies*, but the collection *National Airs* (which includes a very wide diversity of airs from Portugal, Languedoc, Venice, Sicily etc) and is a 'Scottish air'. Moore therefore offers both the possibility of articulating loss, and of translating between diverse identities and histories.

The continual displacement of all of the characters in *The Home Place* demonstrates the impossibility of any authentic home: Ireland's histories are fragmentary and hybrid, marked by the struggle between imperial rule and national resistance, and by economic, social and political inequities. When Margaret realizes that her current position in the Lodge has become impossible after she tells Christopher it is David she loves, she announces that her father will come for her.

She is caught between legacies: that of the Lodge, already a choice of the son over the father, and that of her own father, who though himself in decline through alcohol abuse, is the guardian in turn of the musical legacy of Thomas Moore. Indeed, it is perhaps through the claiming or reclaiming of occluded legacies that *The Home Place* poses the question of home.

There are several other time periods evoked in the play: the moment of planting of the trees of the Lodge, which coincides with the birth of Thomas Moore, so celebrated by the schoolmaster, and, beyond that, the seventh century monastery that Dr Richard Gore visits, a reminder of Irish globalization based on the dissemination of sacred texts and classical study.[24] Margaret informs Richard that the monastery was 'an important centre of learning [...] Some great documents were reproduced there.'[25] As well as different spatial frames, the play offers multiple temporal frameworks, and, as suggested above, multiple legacies. Christopher dreams of escaping 'history and heritage and the awful burden of this (*house*)'.[26] However, what lingers in the mind following the performance is what is not shown on stage, in particular the singing of the children and the monastery's great documents which represent an alternative legacy to the dominant histories of British imperial rule and of militant resistance: 'the doomed nexus of those who believe themselves the possessors and those who believe they're dispossessed'.[27] As in several of Friel's other plays, legacies or inheritances need to be worked through in terms similar to Derrida's concept of inheritance in *Echographies*:

> To inherit is not essentially to receive something, a given that one may then have. It is an active affirmation ... When one inherits, one sorts, one sifts, one reclaims, one reactivates. [...] One selects, one filters, one sifts through ghosts or through the injunctions of each spirit ... If to inherit is to reaffirm an injunction, not simply a possession, but an assignation to be deciphered, then we are only what we inherit.[28]

The spatial and temporal scope of *The Home Place* leaves it little room to flesh out complex characters and interrelationships as in *Dancing at Lughnasa* for example. Indeed when one reads the text after seeing a production, the movements and scope of the characters are predestined – as Mick Gordon noted, every movement is charted and the text and staging choreographed as meticulously as a Beckett play.[29] The play seems to portray its characters as 'specimens' illustrating a dilemma, though reviewers noted that the performances of Ian McElhinney and Aislín McGuckin 'touch the heart'.[30] Perhaps indeed, while masquerading as realism, the play is a contemporary fable posing the question raised by Clement O'Donnell – what kind of songs do we need now at this moment of our history? As the *Variety* review suggested, perhaps the impact of *The Home Place* is less in its moment of performance, than in the lingering injunctions of its ghosts calling us to sift, judge, activate and reclaim our multiple inheritances.

NOTES

[1] Matt Wolf, review of *The Home Place*, *Variety*, 13-19 June 2005: 'There may not be a Friel text with wider resonances to our world at large, even if phrases like 'ethnic cleansing' aren't strictly within the purview of this play. How gratifying to find a writer whose engagement and energies are undimmed by time, even if, dramatically speaking, *The Home Place* doesn't quite hit home.'

[2] Jane Coyle, review of *The Home Place* at the Grand Opera House, Belfast, *Irish Times*, 14 February 2009, p. 14.

[3] Sigmund Freud, 'The Uncanny' in *The Penguin Freud Library*, Volume 14, *Art and Literature* (London & New York: Penguin Books, 1990 (1919)), pp. 335-376.

[4] Homi K. Bhabha, *The Location of Culture* (London: Routledge, 1994), pp. 9-12.

[5] Jacques Derrida, *Specters of Marx: the State of the Debt, the Work of Mourning and the New International*, trans. by Peggy Kamuf (New York and London: Routledge, 1994), p. 16.

[6] Scott Boltwood, *Brian Friel, Ireland and the North* (Cambridge: Cambridge University Press, 2008), p. 206.

[7] At a public seminar at Queen's University on 21st February 2009, Mick Gordon drew attention to Friel's emphasis on the interrelationship between the characters' action, speech and the 'architecture' of the stage.

[8] Brian Friel, *The Home Place* (London: Faber, 2005), p. 37.

[9] Thomas Moore, *The Poetical Works of Thomas Moore* (Philadelphia: Crissy and Thomas, Cowperthwait and Co, 1838), p. 353.

[10] According to A.T. Kearney, Foreign Policy Magazine Globalization Index™, Ireland was top of the list of 62 countries from 2001 – 2004, but slipped to second place in 2005 and fourth in 2006. See <http://www.atkearney.com/main.taf?p=5,4,1,127> [accessed March 2nd 2009].

[11] In stressing the displacements of the planter, *The Home Place* questions the ideology of empire that suggests that the colonizers extend their home into where they are. In *The Expansion of England: Two Courses of Lectures* (London Macmillan, 1883), p. 41, J.R. Seeley states that: 'where Englishmen are there is England, where Frenchmen are, there is France'. Cited in Kenneth Parker, 'To Travel ... Hopefully?', in ed. Liselotte Glage, *Being/s in Transit: Travelling, Migration, Transit* (Amsterdam: Rodopi Press, 2000), p. 24.

[12] Anne McClintock, *Imperial Leather: Race, Gender and Sexuality in the Colonial Contest* (New York & London: Routledge, 1995), p. 5.

[13] Friel, p. 33.

[14] Friel, p. 32.

[15] Friel, p. 24.

[16] David Gore uses this term of his uncle Richard when he describes his measuring techniques: 'Isn't that a little crude' (Friel, p. 29).

[17] Raymond Williams, *Drama in Performance* (Buckingham: Open University Press, 1991 (1968)), p. 126.

[18] Friel, p. 40. In musical terms, measure denotes a unit (sometimes called a bar) which contains a number of beats.

[19] Harry White, *Music and the Irish Literary Imagination* (Oxford: Oxford University Press, 2008), p. 224.

[20] See Ronan Kelly, *Bard of Erin: The Life of Thomas Moore* (Dublin: Penguin Ireland, 2008). Thomas Moore (1779-1852) was born in Aungier Street, Dublin, and was one of the first Catholic students to attend Trinity College Dublin. He was a strong advocate of Catholic Emancipation.

[21] White, p. 50.

[22] White, p. 68.

[23] Matthew Campbell, 'Thomas Moore's Wild Song: The 1821 *Irish Melodies*', *Bullán*, 4:2 (1999), p. 93.

[24] *The Home Place* refers to the monastery as Cistercian (Friel, p. 25), but this seems to be an example of Friel's poetic licence. The Cistercian order was founded in the eleventh century, so the monastery must have been founded by a different order. The seventh century saw the foundation of monasteries such as the Fore Abbey in Westmeath, and the creation of illuminated manuscripts such as the Book of Durrow (begun 650).

[25] Friel, p. 25.

[26] Friel, p. 67.

[27] Friel, p. 71.

[28] Jacques Derrida and Bernard Stiegler, *Echographies of Television*, trans. Jennifer Bajorek (Cambridge UK and Malden US: Polity Press, 2002), pp. 25, 26.

[29] Mick Gordon, public seminar on Friel at Queen's University, 21st February 2009.

[30] Coyle, *op.cit.* Several reviews and features of the 2009 production note that the play has particular resonance in Northern Ireland. See Jane Coyle, 'A Question of Identity', *Irish Times* 3 February 2009, p. 18.

Anna McMullan *is Professor and Chair of Drama at Queen's University Belfast. She has published widely on the work of Samuel Beckett; on Irish theatre; and on the interrelations between gender and performance. Her books include* Theatre on Trial: the Later Drama of Samuel Beckett *(London: Routledge, 1993),* Performing Embodiment in Samuel Beckett *(Routledge, forthcoming), and (with Cathy Leeney)* The Theatre of Marina Carr: Before Rules Was Made *(Dublin: Carysfort Press, 2003).*

# irishtheatre

**MAGAZINE**

**Taking you behind the scenes.**
www.irishtheatremagazine.ie